Media Feedback

Media Feedback

Our Lives in Loops

Ryan Rogers

LEXINGTON BOOKS
Lanham • Boulder • New York • London

Published by Lexington Books
An imprint of The Rowman & Littlefield Publishing Group, Inc.
4501 Forbes Boulevard, Suite 200, Lanham, Maryland 20706
www.rowman.com

6 Tinworth Street, London SE11 5AL, United Kingdom

British Library Cataloguing in Publication Information Available

Library of Congress Control Number: 2021934277

ISBN 978-1-7936-2931-9 (cloth)
ISBN 978-1-7936-2933-3 (pbk)
ISBN 978-1-7936-2932-6 (electronic)

To Meg and Kev.
Your support means everything.

Contents

Contents

Preface

For some time now I have been thinking about this book. A conversation with my niece and nephews emboldened my motivation to write it. They were telling me about some of their favorite video games but so little of what they told me was about the games themselves. There were no descriptions of slaying dragons, beating bosses, and saving the world. Instead, nearly all of the descriptions were related to rewards the kids had earned from playing these games. They described earning virtual money, trading for pets, getting outfits for their avatars, unlocking new types of cars, etc. The genesis of their affinity for these games appeared to be solely based on the feedback systems the games implemented, not the story, the characters, the game play, the graphics, or anything else one might associate with a favorite video game. In a similar conversation, my niece and nephews were telling me about some YouTube videos. Instead of describing the content of the videos to me, they told me how many views and likes the videos had as if those feedback mechanisms somehow validated the content on its face. These kids, more embedded in the media environment than any before them, were obsessed with media feedback even if that is not what they called it.

Feedback is a concept that is simultaneously exalted as extremely powerful but also eludes conceptual understanding and is frequently misapplied practically. Given how much feedback we receive each day from media, it is worthwhile to unpack this concept.

Chapter 1

Feedback, an Elusive Concept

Every day the average person is almost completely surrounded by media feedback, and this feedback influences people in many perceived and unperceived ways. Moreover, the type of media feedback people encounter is constantly changing alongside emergent affordances provided by new technology, websites, and apps. In spite of this, our knowledge of media feedback is quite limited, and thus there is an imperative to develop a deeper understanding of media feedback. In doing so, our society will become more media literate, better understand how we are being influenced, how to implement best practices when creating media, and develop a conceptual foundation for, what this book argues, one of the most important factors in the current media landscape.

Feedback is inherent to nearly every media platform someone encounters. Every like on Facebook, view counted on Instagram, death in a video game, movie suggestion on Netflix, retweet on Twitter, and email reply is a form of media feedback. These are but a few examples. In the current media landscape, people are influenced by feedback more often than not, provided that people have not cut themselves off from media exposure—a task that would require an extreme degree of seclusion.

Despite such omnipresence of media feedback, little research has been done on this topic directly—there is a great deal of research within the orbit of media feedback. The literature will be explored throughout this book as appropriate. The purpose of this book is to provide an overview of media feedback through a series of highly focused empirical studies. Each chapter is designed to explore and test concepts important to media feedback. For example, as some studies have suggested that timeliness is important to feedback, one chapter will be dedicated to testing that premise while another chapter will examine how feedback relevance factors into user perceptions.

More specifically, this book aims to provide a way for readers to understand what media feedback is and how it impacts us each day by dissecting the concept of feedback thoroughly and thoughtfully in each of its critical pieces as dictated by previous research on the topic.

As media has become more "interactive," feedback has become more prevalent. For the purposes of this text, a reader might suggest that media interactivity and media feedback are homogenous or interchangeable and, in some cases, this may be accurate or inaccurate. Thus, interactivity merits further discussion. An understanding of interactivity and how it will be used in this book is essential. "Interactive" is placed in quotes because there are many competing definitions of interactivity such that the concept is difficult to pin down regardless of its ubiquitous use. This book is not interested in parsing those definitions—that would be a book unto itself—but as an example, interactivity has been called "a measure of a media's potential ability to let the user exert an influence on the content and/or form of the mediated communication" (Jensen, 1998, p. 201), control of information flow (Ariely, 2000), a feature or function of technology (Sundar, Kalyanaraman & Brown, 2003), "a process involving users, media, and messages, with an emphasis on how messages relate to one another" (Sundar et al., 2003, p. 34), user perception (Bucy, 2004), as well as speed, mapping, and range in a video game (Reeves & Read, 2013).

This list of definitions is hardly inclusive of the existing definitions of interactivity. There are noteworthy overlaps in some of these definitions but there are also irreconcilable differences between others. For example, one must engage in a degree of mental gymnastics in order to see how interactivity can be both a *feature* of a website and also a user's *perception* of the site. As a result, the term interactivity has become, in part, polluted in the research community, yet it is still widely used in writing. In sum, people know interactivity when they see it but there is not a consensus on what it represents and how interactivity should be defined.

This book does not aim to assert which of these definitions of interactivity is most valid. The point in addressing these differences is twofold. One, what the research community and society broadly understand as interactivity is vital to feedback, and two, interactivity is a concept fraught with confusion and misunderstanding, thus it is not used extensively in this text. In fact, one of the goals of this book is to clarify and unify some of the literature on interactivity by using the concept of feedback in its place. This book argues that the concept of interactivity and the definitions provided earlier can be largely explained through feedback, offering a more parsimonious framework for understanding the media landscape. To be clear, one main assertion made by this book is that when many talk about media interactivity, they are actually talking about media feedback.

Even if media feedback should not completely supplant media interactivity, without a clear conceptualization of interactivity and thus a lack of any possible operationalization, it has been argued that feedback serves writ large as a more useful substitute (Rogers, 2016). Speaking of operationalization, the notion of interactive content creates methodological concerns as detailed in an unpublished manuscript (Rogers, Ivory, Ivory, Keene, & Cipollene, n.d.); consider standard methods of content analysis and experimentation. Interactive content, regardless of definition, refers to user participation in some capacity. As a result, interactive content is ostensibly dynamic by design and ostensibly not uniform based on the individual user. For example, consider the way that content is targeted and filtered for specific Facebook users, a content analysis of the advertisements appearing on Facebook might be radically different depending on who is viewing the content such that a viewer with certain interests and browsing history will encounter different content than another viewer and even different content than a dummy account created for just for the hypothetical project.

Simultaneously, if one wanted to perform an experiment with even some of the most rudimentary, non-contrived video games, there is virtually no way to experimentally control for video game content. For example, one player may breeze through several areas of a game during the experiment while another player might get stuck in one area for the duration of the experiment. This need not account for games with "random" events like multiplayer matches or games that are designed to have a different layout each time such as video games that fall under the "roguelike" genre wherein content is procedurally generated or algorithmically generated. Even a savvy coder who could put participants on a strictly guided path for the purposes of the experiment cannot account for variance in player behavior—if it could, then it would not be a game at all, just a presentation of content without interactivity (there are ways to deceive participants into thinking that they are playing a game but then the manipulation sacrifices generalizability). The confounds that interactivity introduce need to be considered carefully for all experimental research of interactive content. Readers of any paper on this topic should keep this at the top of their minds.

Researchers should question, thoroughly, any research done on interactive content implementing content analysis or experimentation without positively clear conceptualization and operationalization of interactivity. The current standards in the research community are inadequate and, at best, provide an incomplete picture or, at worst, provide inaccurate or misleading information. Again, the argument of this text is that media feedback can provide more useful and clearer methodology for experimentation as well as content analysis than interactivity.

As noted, almost all references to media feedback are contained within some sort of interactive system as described by the current literature. This book suggests that much scholarship has mislabeled media feedback as inter-activity, and this text hopes to correct that classification.

One of the first formal conceptualizations of feedback is as follows (Wiener, 1961, p. 6):

> When we desire a motion to follow a given pattern, the difference between this pattern and the actually performed motion is used as a new input to cause the part regulated to move in such a way as to bring its motion closer to that given by the pattern.

Inherent in Wiener's definition is that feedback is a circular system or a loop (Ashby, 1956; Carver & Scheier, 2001Goetz, 2011). The concept of feedback is often known as a "feedback loop" (Carver & Scheier, 2001; Ramaprasad, 1983) or a "feedback intervention" (Glanz, Schoenfeld, & Steffen, 2010; Haug, Meyer, Ulbricht, Gross, & Rumpf, 2010; Kluger & DeNisi, 1996; Ruiter, Werrij, & de Vries, 2010) but refer to the same core notion.

A feedback loop typically starts with an input value. This can be any sort of data point. This data point is then compared with a goal value—who sets that goal depends on the traits of the feedback loop. From here, there are two possible outcomes—the input value and the goal value are different from one another or the input value and the goal value are the same. In either case, the discrepancy between values, or lack thereof, is communicated back to whatever agent is providing the input value. If the values are the same, then the agent knows (the term "knows" may be convenient but imprecise here as the agent could be a machine, piece of software, or a human being without "knowledge" of the goal or awareness of the feedback loop) it is perform-ing the task correctly, meeting the goal, and continues inputting the same value. If the values are different, then the agent knows it needs to adjust its performance and attempts to input a value closer to the goal value. Ideally, this second input value will be closer to the goal value but if it is not then, the discrepancy will be communicated back to the agent where the agent will "try again" to match the goal value. The same is accurate if an input value that previously matched the goal value deviates from the goal value. The feedback loop will communicate this deviation to the agent in order to correct performance. In any case, this loop is meant to continue in perpetuity until the system is somehow stopped or exited—perhaps the task has been completed or the user gives up on a task.

This definition may seem far afield from media and more applicable to engineering or computing technology. However, feedback has been used in the domain of human behavior. Most commonly in the domain of human behavior, studies argue that feedback is an essential tool in education (Butler

& Winne, 1995; Hattie & Timperlay, 2007; Winne & Butler, 1994). Another area of human behavior that uses feedback frequently is health communication, such that feedback on health is important to producing healthy outcomes for individuals (Hawkins, Kreuter, Resnicow, Fishbein, & Dijkstra, 2008). Feedback is also referenced as useful in counseling or therapy sessions (Thiemann & Goldstein, 2001). Likewise, feedback is referenced in the business sector as a means of improving products and services (Connellan & Zemke, 1993). In sum, the notion of feedback as described by Wiener can and has been applied successfully to human behavior.

While *some* of the literature mentioned may be media feedback it is not necessarily. Again, this highlights the importance of interactivity. Nearly each of the definitions detailed in this chapter can be subsumed by Wiener's (1961) definition of feedback. Regardless, to adopt and interpret the model of a feedback loop fully, the parts of the feedback loop will be discussed specifically in terms of human behavior as that is the most prescient issue. A person's behavior is measured against a goal or standard set by a teacher, a website, a doctor, etc. The discrepancy between the person's behavior and the goal is communicated back to the person so he or she can either maintain his or her current behavior or alter it to reach the goal. Again, this loop continues until the loop is ended or exited.

An article in the technology magazine *Wired* offered a particularly compelling example of feedback's impact on human behavior (Goetz, 2011). The article describes community efforts to lower passing car speeds in school zones. New, bright signs did not work. Increased ticketing of drivers did not work. Eventually, the community arrived at installing dynamic speed displays, a device that tells drivers how fast they are going as compared to the posted speed limit. According to Goetz (2011), these dynamic speed displays reduced speed in school zones by 14 percent and the mean speed in school zones dropped below the posted speed limit. Importantly, these dynamic speed displays did not result in ticketing of drivers; they simply provided information to drivers on their behavior. In other words, drivers were not being punished, they were just educated on their behaviors. They were receiving feedback.

These dynamic speed displays are a strong example of a feedback loop in human behavior and demonstrate the efficacy of feedback broadly. This example can be parsed specifically with regard to the components of a feedback loop. In this case, the input value is how fast the driver/car is traveling. The goal value is the posted speed limit. The dynamic speed displays show the driver the discrepancy or lack thereof between the speed of the car and the posted speed limit (the goal). As a result, drivers were slowing down in order to meet the goal, watching their speed change as they slowed down on the dynamic speed displays.

Media feedback does not function any differently than in the classroom or in a doctor's office; in fact, one could argue that dynamic speed displays are a form of media feedback and that as teacher and doctor feedback are often delivered through mediated platforms today, they are forms of media feedback as well. However, the difference between the existing research and media feedback is the platform through which the feedback loop is implemented. Instead of a therapy session or a meeting with a teacher, media feedback is encountered in mediated environments. Every like on Facebook, view counts on Instagram, death in a video game, movie suggestion on Netflix, retweet on Twitter, is an attempt to create a feedback loop with a user while intending to guide that user's next input. Whether or not it is effective is another question unto itself which will be explored in detail throughout this text. One person might be highly motivated by seeing his or her tweet retweeted or liked while that may not matter to another person. How much a tweet is liked or retweeted will inform how one person tweets and interacts with the website subsequently. In a video game, if a player is repeatedly dying, then he or she knows that he or she must alter his or her inputs, try different strategies or tactics, level up, or try exploring a different area. Barring individual differences, the quality of the media feedback loop will inform how effective an individual will be in producing an input that matches the goal value on the mediated platform.

Another important consideration is who is setting the goal value in media feedback loops. Generally, there are two key parties setting goals in media feedback. One is the content producer or organization that owns the media platform. For example, a website may have a goal of increasing user time on a site or the number of sales made from a site. Thus, the goal value is determined by the media organization and they should set up a feedback loop to optimize these behaviors.

The other goal-setters are the users themselves. Users enter a media feedback loop with their own goals in mind. A user may use a website in order to reach certain goals he or she had set for him or herself. For example, a user might want to increase his or her number of followers or raise money on a crowdfunding site for a local charity. The goals can be as varied as the individuals themselves. Sometimes these goals are antisocial, trolling intended to incite controversy or provoke negative emotional reactions, and attacking people personally on social media platforms.

Regardless of the goal for the user and the platform, what is important is that these goals are often symbiotic such that the design of a site will help the media organization reach its goal while also allowing the user to work toward his or her goal. There can be two or more feedback loops operating simultaneously. This is then multiplied when multiple users are included on one platform. This multitude of feedback loops creates a more complex landscape than trying to get drivers to slow down. When the two or more feedback loops work together, feedback can become an even more powerful tool, but this is not always the case. For instance, a website's design or a user's actions may actually hinder the goals of an individual or the media organization in which case neither media organization nor the individual is able to satisfactorily implement a feedback loop and reach their goals.

Regardless of who is setting the goal value, media organization or user, a valuable framework for examining media feedback is the media effects tradition. Media effects broadly refer to the area of study that examines how media content influences the attitudes and behaviors of the people who consume them. Throughout this text, a variety of theories and concepts subsumed under the media effects umbrella will be implemented as appropriate. The position of this book is that many of these theories and concepts are useful for understanding media feedback or aspects of media feedback by seeing which might apply and which might not.

To further elucidate the particular relevance of feedback, the conceptualizations of interactivity in this chapter are dissected through the lens of feedback. Each of the conceptualizations of interactivity detailed in this chapter can be reframed and *simplified* in terms of media feedback.

Jensen (1998, p. 201) states, "A measure of a media's potential ability to let the user exert an influence on the content and/or form of the mediated communication." Jensen goes on to describe differing levels of interactivity. In each case, Jensen indicates that user control is vital to interactivity. In the context of this text, Jensen's notion of control can be understood as user input such that a user controls the input that he or she provides in a feedback loop.

When interactivity is discussed in terms of control of information flow (Ariely, 2000), the idea is that a user can engage in dynamic heterogeneity or the ability to fluidly generate and test hypotheses while using a website, for example. Using the lens of feedback, Ariely is describing the essence of a media feedback loop wherein the goal value is determined by the user and, thus, the user exerts control by setting the goal value for him or herself. For example, a person might look for information on a recent news story on a website, setting a goal value for a feedback loop. As people peruse different sites and stories, they judge how accurately previously used inputs meet their goals and recalibrate search terms to better accommodate the goals.

Two more definitions of interactivity will be discussed in conjunction: the functional view of interactivity and the contingency view of interactivity (Sundar et al., 2003). The functional view states, "Increased interactivity simply translates to an interface's capacity for conducting a dialogue or information exchange between users and the interface" (Sundar et al., 2003, p. 3). In other words, the more interactive features a platform has, the more interactive it is provided that the features allow for dialogue between user and interface. The contingency view of interactivity states that interactivity is "a process involving users, media, and messages, with an emphasis on how messages relate to one another" (Sundar et al., 2003, p. 34). These two views are presented as competing, but through the lens of feedback they can be reconciled as one parsimonious concept. Taken together, the contingency view and the functional view of interactivity fundamentally describe media feedback. Without contingent dialogue, feedback does not exist. Without features that provide information, feedback does not exist. The degree of interactivity, both functional and contingent, can be understood as the quality of the feedback loop. This loop could be information rich or information poor. This becomes a question of feedback quality, not whether or not this is feedback itself.

Looking at video games specifically, Reeves and Read (2013) suggest that interactivity is based on the time it takes for a game to respond to input, the match between actions in the mediated space and actions in the physical world like one swinging his or her arm to bowl in a bowling video game as opposed to simply pressing a button, and the number of different responses as a result of input. The term "input" is used frequently in this conceptualization. Input is a vital part of a feedback loop.

Perhaps the most broadly useful definition of interactivity is Bucy's (2004) argument that interactivity is based on user perception. In other words, interactivity is not a feature of a platform but simply what a person *feels* when using a media platform. Ultimately, Bucy suggests that we do not have an adequate body of knowledge of interactivity yet and thus conceptualizations should be treated with caution. The current text agrees with this sentiment and suggests that feedback is a practical stand-in for interactivity. Indeed, the same notion Bucy employs can be applied to feedback such that media feedback might be viewed through the user's perceptions while in a feedback loop.

Implied throughout this chapter is that feedback is important. Previous and recent research indicates that feedback is critical to the function of many different processes. In teaching, feedback from an instructor is considered "very important" (Hu, 2019). Indeed, feedback on writing is important for students but very time-consuming for instructors and so mediated platforms have been developed to alleviate instructor workload without losing valued information for students (Stevenson & Phakiti, 2019). In robotic and software systems, feedback is critical for the systems to function properly (Westervelt, Grizzle, Chevallereau, Choi, & Morris, 2018; Zamir, Wu, Sun, Shen, Shi, Malik, & Savarese, 2017). In fact, feedback is "crucial; in some situations [poor or lack of feedback] may lead to a catastrophe instead of an improvement in the system behavior" (Ozbay, 2019, p.1).

Specific to media, feedback can influence user behavior online (Burrow & Rainone, 2017) and businesses need to solicit and consider consumer feedback in order to create successful products (Deng, Franke, Hribernik, & Thoben, 2017). In short, feedback is important and influential and should be accepted as a primary assumption of this book. Media feedback demands our attention in particular because of the way our media landscape is constantly evolving, giving us new types of feedback loops influencing us in predictable and unforeseen ways. Likewise, this book should be considered a call to action to explore this promising concept in mediated environments, in order to avoid confusion and unnecessary complexity found with other concepts concerning human-computer interaction.

Many disciplines have determined that feedback is a useful concept for exploring those respective fields, but this has led to multiple references to feedback, many of which are confusing, inconsistent, or outright conflicting. This section will outline some of those viewpoints and provide conceptual clarity in order to codify our understanding of feedback and thereby enhance its applicability. This should provide guidance on how to best and appropriately use feedback as it has been misused considerably in the academic literature published to date.

As noted, the origin of feedback can be traced back to engineering but has since been employed in biological sciences, business, economics, cybernetics, ecology, chemistry, robotics, and human behavior (Bowlby, 1969; Goetz, 2011; Miller, Galanter, & Pribram, 1960; Mindell, 2003; Ozbay, 2019; Senge, 1990; Westervelt et al., 2018). This broad spectrum of application alone can confer the broad value of feedback. If feedback has managed to find purchase in so many of these disparate disciplines, then it is at least noteworthy, even vital, beyond the scope of this book. Not many concepts can claim such a distinction.

Alongside this breadth of application, the concept has become muddled and, understandably, what is most germane to engineers may not be most germane to social scientists. Consequently, the concept of feedback has been applied in various ways or certain aspects of feedback have received more attention than others. As a result, feedback does not have a clear conceptualization in certain instances or at least does not reflect Wiener's original definition, (1961) which should be used as clear guidelines when implementing and discussing feedback.

The term "feedback" is used haphazardly in academic research. Very few studies provide clear conceptualizations of feedback even when it is a key concept to the study. Unsurprisingly, many such studies misuse feedback. On this point, feedback is a term that is in common parlance such that people discuss it without much regard for its meaning, as such many authors may not feel that they need to define it in their work. In other studies, researchers often discuss feedback without realizing it and do not mention feedback by name leaving the reader to infer that feedback is a central concept in the piece.

Beyond this, terminology is not uniform. Some studies only use the term feedback (Burrow & Rainone, 2017; Butkowski, Dixon, Weeks, & Smith, 2019; Sabik, Falat, & Magagnos, 2019), other times, the terms "feedback loop" (Carver & Scheier, 2001; Ramaprasad, 1983),"feedback intervention," (Glanz, Schoenfeld, & Steffen, 2010; Haug, Meyer, Ulbricht, Gross, & Rumpf, 2010; Kluger & DeNisi, 1996; Ruiter, Werrij, & de Vries, 2010) or "feedback system" (Heinen, Heuser, Steinschulte, & Walther, 2017; Wang, Katzschmann, Teng, Araki, Giarré, & Rus, 2017) are used.

While they all broadly refer to the same *idea* there are differences between them. The clearest distinction is between the terms that suggest a process (feedback loop, feedback intervention, feedback system) versus the simple term feedback which implies a piece of information. For example, consider a student taking an exam. The student receives a grade of 80 percent, on the exam. This piece of information is useful to the student as it communicates that he or she did well but did not master the content. This is how most people tend to think of feedback—a piece of information given to someone after the performance of a task. In this case, the information on the behavior is commonly referred to as feedback.

However, this view of feedback is myopic and limiting for the purposes of understanding media. Viewing feedback as one-time information on a performance, in this case, a grade on an exam, ignores all of the preparation for the exam and anything that happens after the exam as a result of the feedback. Taking a macro perspective of feedback using the exam score as an example, there is much more to examine, unpack, and elaborate upon. The first of these is the student input on the exam. This would be the student's responses to exam questions. The student's preparation before the exam *should* be guided by previous assessments of the student's work by the instructor and the student's self-assessment, provided that the student is taking responsibility for his or her education and the instructor is performing his or her educational duties. Asking students to take exams without some form of assessment beforehand is unfair to them.

Second, the student input is evaluated based on a standard. In this case, answers would be marked correct or incorrect. An evaluator, whether by instructor, teaching assistant, or automated grading software, judges the input.

Third, the percentage of correct answers is communicated back to the student. This can take any number of shapes, a score posted online, a written explanation, handing back the completed exam to the student, etc. Please note that viewing feedback as one-time information on a behavior *only* accounts for this step.

Finally, the student can calibrate his or her behavior afterward in order to accommodate this new information. If the student is satisfied with an 80 percent then he or she will likely maintain current behaviors. If the student is not satisfied with this score then he or she may work with the instructor or alter study techniques so subsequent inputs are more accurate and better grades are received.

Treating feedback as a piece of information is quite common and, in many cases, much simpler than looking at feedback from a broader perspective. However, feedback, as originally conceptualized, does not occur in a vacuum such as this. The most important thing to consider is that treating feedback as a piece of information ignores upstream and downstream attributes of that piece of information that are endemic to feedback.

This book argues that defining feedback as a process is more relevant to understanding media feedback from a conceptual perspective. Sometimes, in order to make the concept of feedback more manageable and to easily operationalize it in a study, the scope of feedback may be limited to create experimental control. Indeed, when looking at human behavior, if an extreme macro approach is taken, then feedback could include the entire lifespan of an individual which would be nearly impossible to study empirically. Placing parameters on the process of feedback is essential. That is why it is critical to clearly define and understand what feedback loop is of interest as this allows for more realistic and accurate constraints to be placed on a project.

As for media feedback this is particularly germane, relationships with media platforms are often ongoing and not limited to one piece of information. For example, some have maintained social media profiles for years. As such, the process view of feedback is much more appropriate than the information view, though the loop should be thoughtfully selected (session, hours, day, week, post, reply, etc.) For example, Spotify is a popular music streaming service. Part of the service is known as the "daily mix" comprised of songs that the service generates based on the user's previous listening patterns. The idea is that through the previous listening behaviors, or inputs, a playlist can be constructed for the specific user that will likely be valued by the user. In other words, if someone listens to a lot of hip hop and also bluegrass music, Spotify can make playlists that accommodate both of these seemingly disparate genre preferences because the user has demonstrated interest in both of those genres. Simultaneously, the mixes are not likely to include heavy metal because the user has not demonstrated a preference for this genre through inputs on the platform. Spotify's goal, in all likelihood, is to provide a product that users are happy with and thus continue using the service or even become willing to pay for the service. The more one uses Spotify, the more Spotify can use data points to create these daily mixes that cater to individual taste. Thus, a media feedback loop is created.

Conceptually, if feedback is limited to a piece of information, then it would be limited to the daily mix at one point in time but the daily mix is a living, dynamic set of content that is repeatedly influenced by user input. Surely, a daily mix made after 15 minutes with Spotify would be much more constrained in its ability to appeal to a user than a daily mix that has been built over a year of user inputs. This suggests that the feedback on Spotify is more than just a piece of information but an in-depth process that exists across sessions and multiple actions from the user and the platform.

Given this example and a preference for the process view of feedback, examining Spotify as a feedback mechanism is useful. When a person uses Spotify, they enter that feedback loop. When the person stops using Spotify, they still exist in that loop but can reenter at any time.

Notably, the terms "loop" and "system" indicate that some portion of the process is automated. For a feedback loop to exist and to be effective, there needs to be some degree of systematic evaluation and/or self-regulation. Spotify, presumably, uses data aggregation and algorithms to make its daily mixes. According to its website, they "include your regular listens" and "songs we think you'll love." As for daily mixes, "the more you listen, the more frequently it updates" (Spotify.com, 2020). While not explicitly stated, the website describes a feedback loop that regulates itself based on how users interact with it. It also describes the process as ongoing, not a one-time interaction. In fact, the site suggests that the more a user inputs, the more robust the feedback loop and the better the product. This is vital not only to Spotify's business model but to the concept of feedback itself. Circling back to the notion of automation or self-regulation, even the score on an exam is automated in a sense—answers are either correct or incorrect. The feedback loop of an exam, while it may be graded by hand, has an answer key or grading rubric intended to self-regulate the process. Notably, qualitative information can be used in a feedback loop as well but subjectivity inside a feedback loop makes it more complex and sometimes more difficult to understand (Stevenson & Phakiti, 2019).

In review, feedback is often used to refer to pieces of information rather than a process, particularly in media research and human behavior research. This error is less common in other disciplines such as robotics, biology, and cybernetics. Feedback is more useful and more accurately described when thought of as a process.

Besides confusing feedback for information instead of process, one of the most common discrepancies found in feedback literature is the use of "positive" feedback and "negative" feedback. There is a lack of consistency within the feedback literature regarding how these terms are used. Moreover, the implementations are conceptually distinct and add more confusion to research on feedback. On the one hand, positive and negative feedback have been defined in terms of information on performance evaluation and the corresponding emotional valence such that positive feedback (performing well) elicits positive emotions and negative feedback (performing poorly) provides negative emotions (Burrow & Rainone, 2017; Carnagey & Anderson, 2005; Connellan & Zemke, 1993; Deng et al., 2017; Hattie & Timperley, 2007; Reinecke, et al., 2012). Under this paradigm, positive feedback is, "you did very well, keep up the good work" and negative feedback is, "you did poorly, you should try harder next time." These types of studies tend to view feedback as information instead of process, though not exclusively.

Not surprisingly, feedback in the form of information on negative performance evaluations has different effects on individuals than positive information on performance evaluations (Carnagey & Anderson, 2005; Hattie & Timperley, 2007; Reinecke et al., 2012) and the current text is careful to note that these are information on performance evaluations, not feedback as a process. Information on performance evaluations can be part of feedback but to treat this as feedback prima facie is inaccurate.

In media feedback research, this mistake is made often. Burrow and Rainone (2017) suggest that the feedback affordances on Facebook influence self-esteem because positive feedback indicates acceptance by others. This study makes two errors, first, it adopts a functional view of feedback and, second, it labels information on performance evaluation as feedback. Sabik and colleagues (2019) make similar errors. In their study on psychological well-being and social media use, they mischaracterize positive feedback in the same fashion. To be fair to these authors, they cite previous work that has also mischaracterized feedback (Brooks, 2015; Smith et al., 2008; Valkenburg et al., 2006) and there are even studies that predate these that mischaracterize positive feedback such that there is a tradition of mischaracterizing feedback in the academic community. In the domain of media, the notion of positive and negative feedback has been mishandled almost universally. One aim of this book is to correct this error as it ignores foundational literature on feedback, creates discord between disciplines, and perpetuates existing confusion on the topic.

Traditionally, positive and negative feedback refers to the orientation in which the input is directed with regard to the discrepancy between the input value and the goal value (Ramaprasad, 1983; Carver & Scheier, 2001). Notably, this has *no direct relevance* to the perceived emotional valence of a piece of information on performance evaluation. In this tradition, positive feedback drives the input values *away* from a specific value while negative feedback *reduces* the discrepancy between the input values and a specific value. In other words, positive feedback is designed to make the discrepancy between an input and a goal value *larger* or greater while negative feedback is designed to make the value of the discrepancy between input value and goal value a smaller number, thus chipping away at a larger original input value.

In media studies, this distinction could also be discerned from an approach/ avoid perspective (Carver & Scheier, 2001; Ramaprasad, 1983). Approach information works to funnel performances toward a goal by telling users which actions to pursue. Avoid information pushes performances away from an undesired state. Carnagey and Anderson (2005) illustrated this distinction by offering study participants a positive performance evaluation through point accrual or a negative performance evaluation through point deduction for harming pedestrians in a video game. Players changed their play style based on whether or not they were encouraged to approach or avoid this behavior.

This is a more accurate and useful way of thinking about feedback orientation. When positive/negative feedback is regarded in terms of emotional valence its application is limited. For example, if a person gives a machine feedback in terms of positive emotional valence, the machine will not attribute emotional value to the input in the same way that a person would, unless dealing with some sort of advanced artificial intelligence. Even then, the emotional value of the feedback might depend on scripts or algorithms rather than actual emotion. On this point, when positive/negative feedback is regarded in terms of emotional valence, it assumes how people will respond to positive and negative feedback. For some people, negative feedback might actually be more motivating than positive feedback.

Imagine an "ugly duckling" effect wherein someone is repeatedly given negatively valenced emotional feedback only to overcome the emotional negativity to succeed at the task he or she was so discouraged from initially. For example, a student might need to be told to "be better" or "try harder" in order to feel motivated. Likewise, someone may prefer negatively valenced emotional feedback as it has a greater likelihood of being constructive. A gifted art student who wishes to master a certain technique may not appreciate being told that he or she is wonderful when he or she would prefer to be guided toward improvement through criticism.

Conversely, positively valenced emotional feedback might be perceived as inauthentic. If a video game tells a player that he or she is doing well but that information does not accurately reflect how the player feels or how the player is actually performing—if the player has failed multiple times, for example—then the positively valenced emotional feedback would likely be discredited and viewed as disingenuous or inappropriately effusive. When positive/negative feedback is regarded in terms of emotional valence, studies tend to assume that positively valenced emotional feedback is good and negatively valenced emotional feedback is bad but the reality is much more complex than that. As a result, the approach/avoid paradigm is more useful and consistent.

Based on this, this book advocates for an approach/avoid view of feedback, not a positive/negative view. Beyond removing the complexity of positive and negative emotions associated with feedback, the approach/avoid view of feedback expands the use of feedback such that it can be used to alter inputs in two separate ways (approach and avoid). When positive/negative feedback is regarded in terms of emotional valence, the direction of that feedback is either unclear or pushes inputs in one direction. Moreover, the approach/avoid view is more useful when thinking about mediated systems that do not register emotion. This view provides a more accurate picture of media feedback but perhaps most importantly, positive/negative feedback regarded in terms of emotional valence can be subsumed by the approach/avoid view. If readers are not convinced by this argument, consider that negatively valenced emotional feedback could be viewed as avoid feedback (e.g., "do not do this") while positively valenced emotional feedback could be viewed as approach feedback (e.g., "keep doing this").

Using the approach/avoid view of feedback makes conceptualization and operationalization more flexible and more precise than using an emotional lens.

Another area of discussion in the existing literature is implicit and explicit feedback. Media are often designed to guide users' behaviors without users necessarily being aware of the gentle hand at their backs. Being told explicitly what to do by a media platform might be unappealing or feel manipulative but being given enough of an implicit guide can be very rewarding. Alternatively, a clueless user might want more explicit feedback.

Juul (2010) describes all of the implicit feedback at work in the video game *Guitar Hero* as an example of effective feedback. *Guitar Hero*, when playing, does not interrupt the player and tell him or her exactly what to do to improve performance. However, it does offer a multitude of cues to tell the player whether or not he or she is failing or succeeding such as the screen flashing colors, the crowd cheering, and recognizable songs playing. These cues tell the player what to do implicitly without telling him or her *explicitly* what to do. Explicit instruction would likely make the game considerably less enjoyable and it would have not been the phenomenon that it was in the 2000s. Notably, these pieces of information do serve as performance evaluation, but it is part of an ongoing process that makes it feedback rather than a single piece of information.

On the other hand, if a user is new to Snapchat, explicit feedback would likely be welcomed by the user. The interface could guide the user with precision and expertise that might not be intuitive for a first-time user. In this case, a user might desire explicit feedback over implicit feedback so he or she can learn and use the app more efficiently.

Consider the product ratings and reviews on Amazon.com which uses both implicit and explicit feedback. Provided that there are many reviews of a product, the star rating and comments explicitly show users' input on the site. Simultaneously, Amazon.com is using implicit feedback when it suggests products that may be relevant to the user or products that the user had viewed in the past. Amazon.com does not explicitly state to the user "buy these products," but it is attempting to guide purchasing behavior through these implicit cues.

Implicit feedback may not always be as easy to interpret or understand as explicit feedback but despite these challenges some researchers have suggested that implicit feedback can be easier and cheaper to aggregate (Joachims et al. 2017). These researchers examined how a user's rank of relevance differed from eye-tracking data where a user's rank was viewed as explicit feedback and eye-tracking data was viewed as implicit feedback.

None of this to say that one is better or more effective than the other. This is simply descriptive, so readers have a clear understanding of the types of feedback described in the academic literature.

This chapter only scratches the surface on some of the applications of feedback. However, these are some of the most common viewpoints taken on feedback in the academic literature. Thus, this chapter should be useful in not only illuminating those viewpoints but in helping to guide best practices with regard to feedback.

Feedback can be parsed further in many ways and it should be. It is a useful concept in many different domains. Some of the iterations building on the current knowledge of feedback are quite compelling and worth noting here to show applications that are currently being explored. One study examined how cultural backgrounds influence the feedback process (Hu, 2019). This is an important question in the research community as western, individualistic cultures may react differently than eastern, collectivist cultures. Zamir and colleagues (2017) examined the benefits of feedback rather than feedforward. Deng and colleagues (2017) argued that customer feedback is essential to product development and are careful to describe a closed loop for Product Lifecycle Management. Similarly, Ozbay (2019) argued for feedback control theory wherein the controller of feedback is the most vital component of how feedback works. Without getting into too much depth related to these studies, the point is that feedback is a fruitful area of study, but there is a need for researchers to have a cohesive and uniform view of feedback. Without this, studies on media feedback should be approached with skepticism and a critical eye. The remainder of this book is dedicated to this idea. Each chapter is designed to empirically test different aspects of feedback and assumptions made about feedback.

Chapter 2

Measures and Recruitment

The majority of the remainder of this book consists of empirical studies on media feedback. Many of these studies use similar measures and/or a similar recruitment strategy in order to allow for comparison of studies between chapters. Rather than duplicate the measures and recruitment strategy in each chapter, this chapter serves as an explanation of measures and recruitment strategy used broadly throughout the book. Wording of the measures may be adapted slightly in order to accommodate the study specific to that chapter but the measures are all consistent in terms of where they are adapted from. If the measurements and recruitment strategies differ significantly from the ones detailed in this chapter, it is noted specifically in that respective chapter.

Doing this allows for comparisons between chapters such that the study in one chapter is consistent enough with another study in another chapter. This makes the book more than a collection of disparate studies but a series of studies that provide more detail on the phenomenon of media feedback. This also allows for a unifying look at all of the different variables and why they might be important for understanding media feedback.

MEASURES

The following measures were selected as they are most germane to understanding media feedback.

First, feelings of *entertainment*, *enjoyment*, and *meaningfulness* are critical measures when examining user-end experiences with media. Most media are designed to entertain audiences in some capacity. Media's capacity for impact on audiences in many ways is dependent on its ability to entertain. In other words, if media is not entertaining, then people will not consume it and thus will be rendered moot. This is a notion well-established in media research couched in the media effects tradition of scholarship (Ruggiero, 2000). In this vein, scholars have suggested that media entertainment can be both enjoyable and meaningful (Oliver et al., 2016; Oliver & Bartsch, 2010, Oliver & Raney, 2011; Rogers, 2018; Rogers et al., 2017). More specifically, the suggestion is that something can be entertaining because it is enjoyable, meaningful, or a combination of the two. When something is enjoyable it tends to be more hedonic like a raucous comedy film. When something is considered meaningful, it tends to provide insight into the human condition or provide an understanding of life truths such as a tragic movie that documents the profound struggles of its characters. Both are entertaining but the source of the entertainment is enjoyment, meaningfulness, or both.

In this book, feelings of *entertainment, enjoyment,* and *meaningfulness* are all single-item measures on 7-point Likert-type scale where 1 represents "strongly disagree" and 7 represents "strongly agree." The statements are, "I was entertained by this," "I enjoyed this," and "I found this meaningful," respectively. While the use of single-item measures is not ideal and there are scales for entertainment, enjoyment, and meaningfulness, single-item measures were selected in order to shorten the questionnaires to reduce respondent fatigue where possible. On top of this, single-item measures for these concepts are viable, and there are valid arguments for using single-item measures effectively (Bergkvist & Rossiter, 2007; Wanous, Reichers, & Hudy, 1997). For the most part, these three variables—entertainment, enjoyment, and meaningfulness—are treated as main outcomes throughout the book.

From there many other variables were measured and were broadly treated as potential mediator variables for the outcome variables. These were selected carefully based on existing research on feedback and other studies on media use, which are detailed as they are introduced. Specifically, these variables reflect key concepts related to feedback as described in chapter 1. *Competence, autonomy,* and *relatedness* were measured. These three components comprise self-determination theory (SDT) (Ryan & Deci, 2000). SDT is a theory of intrinsic motivation such that the more an individual feels competent, autonomous, and strong relationships, the more he or she will be intrinsically motivated to perform a task related to those feelings. This theory has been fruitful in the exploration of media consumption and deepens the exploration of media effects. To state plainly within the realm of media, the more media content engenders feelings of competence, autonomy, and relatedness, the more the media experience will be liked and appreciated by the user (Oliver et al., 2016). These variables have shown to be viable in a variety of studies on media (Oliver et al., 2016; Ryan, Rigby, & Przybylski, 2006; Tamborini et al., 2010). As such, the current book on media feedback uses these variables in nearly all of the chapters. Competence is comprised of three items: "I felt competent (knowledgeable) using this media," "I felt very capable and effective using this media," and "I felt like I had the ability to perform the tasks asked of me." Autonomy was comprised of three items: "I felt like I had a lot of options while using this media," "I felt like I had a lot of freedom while using this media," and "I was able to do things with this media because they interested me." Relatedness was comprised of three items: "I found the relationships I formed with this media fulfilling," "I felt like I was part of a group using this media," and "I felt like I was part of a community when using this media." Each was measured on a 7-point Likert-type scale where 1 represented "strongly disagree" and 7 represented "strongly agree."

Cognitive load was measured using the NASA Task Load Index (Hart, & Staveland, 1988). This measure included six items: "How mentally demanding was the task?" "How physically demanding was the task?" "How hurried or rushed was the pace of the task?" "How successful were you in accomplishing what you were asked to do?" (reverse coded), "How hard did you have to work to accomplish your level of performance?" and "How insecure, discouraged, irritated, stressed, and annoyed were you?" Each was measured on a 7-point Likert-type scale where 1 represented "not at all" and 7 represented "very much so." Cognitive load is important to studies on media feedback because people feel different levels of cognitive load when receiving feedback (Campbell & Kirmani, 2000). If media feedback leads to states wherein cognitive capacity is overloaded, then users enter an unpleasant psychological state (Mayer and Moreno, 2003).

Another element endemic in feedback literature is whether or not it has a negative or positive emotional valence. Please do not confuse the importance of how someone feels about feedback with defining feedback by this standard. How people feel about feedback is important to its function but should not be central in how it is defined. Here, instead of an umbrella good or bad emotion, this book narrows the concept to measure whether or not the feedback was encouraging or discouraging. Presumably, for feedback to be effective in eliciting behavior change, it should be more encouraging than discouraging. A media feedback mechanism likely to want users to feel positive about their ability to accomplish a task as opposed to negative about their ability to accomplish a task. These were measured with one item each: "I found the media discouraging" and "I found the media encouraging." Each was measured on a 7-point Likert-type scale where 1 represented "strongly disagree" and 7 represented "strongly agree."

Ramaprasad (1983) notes that the *frequency* of feedback needs to be optimized to enhance performance and the effect of frequency is likely curvilinear such that feedback can be either too infrequent or too frequent. As a result, one item assessing frequency was used, "I found that the feedback provided was frequent." This was measured on a 7-point Likert-type scale where 1 represented "strongly disagree" and 7 represented "strongly agree."

In terms of media use, *surveillance* was also assessed using three items adapted from Lee and Schoenstedt (2011). Items included, "The media provided me with quick and easy access to large volumes of information," "I was able to obtain a wide range of information," and "I learned about things happening in the world." Each was measured on a 7-point Likert-type scale where 1 represented "strongly disagree" and 7 represented "strongly agree." This was included because information acquisition is central to the function of a feedback loop. Also, Brown and colleagues (2018) indicate that this is a motivation for media consumption broadly.

In a study examining website user satisfaction (Muylle, Moenaert, & Despontin, 2004), information traits were viewed as integral. This is also applicable to media feedback. Information quality should be an important factor regarding the efficacy of media feedback. As a result, *information accuracy, information comprehensibility, information comprehensiveness,* and *information relevance* were adapted from Muylle and colleagues (2004). Information accuracy included, "The information is accurate," "The information is not precise" (reverse coded), and "I can rely on the information." Information comprehensibility included, "The information is easy to understand, "The information is clear to me, "The information is presented clearly," and "The information is not presented in an adequate way" (reverse coded). Information comprehensiveness included, "It provides sufficient information," "The information is complete," and "The information is sufficiently detailed." Information relevance included, "The information is relevant," "The information is to the point," and "The information does not help me at all" (reverse coded). Each was measured on a 7-point Likert-type scale where 1 represented "strongly disagree" and 7 represented "strongly agree."

In each chapter additional measures were added, but those are detailed in those studies.

PARTICIPANT RECRUITMENT

Participants were recruited from Amazon.com's Mechanical Turk service. They were offered U.S.$0.25 to participate in each study as this amount was commensurate with similar tasks on Mechanical Turk. While using an online service such as Mechanical Turk reduces lab oversight, best practices were employed in order to improve data quality (Buhrmester, Kwang, & Gosling, 2011 Sheehan, 2018; Veksler & Boren, 2017). Specifically, participants were required to have an approval rate (%) that was greater than or equal to 90, their location had to be in the United States, and they had to have been approved for fifty or more tasks on Mechanical Turk—meaning that they were not new to the process. Also, the questionnaire itself had several attention checks and many items were reverse coded to ensure that participants were paying attention. Specifically, questions were embedded that required the participant to respond in specific ways. If participants failed these attention checks, they were removed from the analysis.

ANALYSIS

Given the general uniformity in data collection, the analysis was also uniform. Again, this allowed for comparison across chapters.

First, if the chapter used an experiment, a multivariate analysis of variance was performed using the experimental condition specific to each chapter as the independent variable and all of the variables listed here as dependent variables. Second, provided there were significant results, the variables were entered into the Process (Hayes, 2018) macro in order to test for mediation. Third, if there was no experiment, a hierarchical regression was used as the previous analysis would not be viable. Logically, a hierarchical regression then must be done in each chapter, even those with experiments, in order to allow for comparison across chapters as this gave the most uniform results across all chapters. While this analysis may seem redundant and unnecessary in certain chapters, it was still performed in order to allow for a macro view of feedback.

Chapter 3

Approach and Avoid Feedback

Given the particular import and confusion in the literature regarding approach/ avoid feedback and positive/negative feedback detailed previously, the next two chapters provide empirical evidence that the concepts are distinct and should be treated as such. This chapter focuses on the difference between approach feedback and avoid feedback while the next chapter will examine positively/negatively valenced emotional feedback.

One noteworthy way to think about approach and avoid feedback in the domain of media feedback is from a theoretical perspective of framing, specifically gain and loss frames. "Framing is among the most heavily referenced paradigms used to guide communication research, and gain-loss framing is among the most frequently employed framing strategies across a wide variety of communication contexts" (Nabi et al., 2019, p. 1-2) including media feedback. Framing refers to how a media message is presented to an audience, which points are included, which points are excluded, the underlying issues etc. (Nelson, Clawson, & Oxley, 1997). In Nelson and colleagues' study, participants read a news article about a Ku Klux Klan rally. One group read a story that framed the rally as a public disturbance while another group read a story that framed the rally as a matter of free speech. Those who read the article that framed the rally as a matter of free speech reported more tolerance of the Ku Klux Klan than those who read the story that framed the rally as a public disturbance. In sum, content creators can influence user attitudes and opinions based on how they frame their content.

Extending from this line of inquiry is the notion of gain or loss frames. Typically, gain framed messages focus on benefits, achievements, and attainment of certain desirable states while loss framed messages focus on negative or damaging states (Rothman & Salovey, 1997). Often, gain and loss frames are used in health communication research and practice (Nabi et al., 2019).

For example, a person with diabetes can receive a message about the benefits of using treatment as prescribed (gain frame) or they can receive a message about the hazards of ignoring the doctor's instructions (loss frame).

In many ways, healthcare can be viewed as a feedback loop unto itself. When someone feels sick, his or her body is telling the individual to act in a way that will improve his or her current condition. When someone feels well, his or her body is telling the individual to continue acting in this fashion to maintain that condition. A doctor's visit is similar. A doctor may prescribe a treatment, and then on a follow-up appointment, the doctor is likely to give feedback to the patient on how the treatment is working. These examples of healthcare feedback do not, by definition, have a media component but that is changing rapidly given the use of online patient portals, telehealth, and wearable devices that give health-related feedback to their wearers (Fowler, 2020; Marketwatch, 2020). This is something that certainly merits further exploration.

Undeniably, gain and loss frames have a clear application to health communication, but they can also be applied in any number of ways including to other media. Consider promotional emails one might receive on a daily basis. One email might say "don't miss out on this limited-time offer" while another email says, "take advantage of these great deals." They are both promoting sales and encouraging specific consumer behavior, but one is presenting the sale event as a loss (missing out) and the other is presenting it as a gain (taking advantage).

Conceptually, gain and loss frames have been treated as distinct from approach and avoid feedback but there are noteworthy overlaps that may help bridge media feedback and this common framing device. In gain frames, message recipients are being pushed toward certain behaviors. In loss frames, message recipients are being pushed away from certain behaviors. In other words, messages try to get participants to avoid a loss or attain a gain. To rephrase in terms of approach and avoid feedback, in gain frames, message recipients are being instructed to approach certain behavioral states and in loss frames, message recipients are being instructed to avoid certain behavioral states. As a reminder, approach feedback tries to get inputs closer to a goal value while avoid feedback tries to keep inputs away from certain values. Thus, the conjecture of this chapter is that much of the work done on gain and loss frames can be used to help understand approach and avoid feedback or at the very least provide an orientation for understanding the two different types of feedback in more established literature. When dealing with media, approach and avoid feedback is not all that different than gain and loss frames as such there is no need to reinvent the wheel with regard to this concept.

With this in mind, consider a metanalysis by Nabi and colleagues (2019) that found across thirty years of study, gain frames tend to be associated with positive emotions and loss frames tend to be associated with negative emotions. A similar pattern should be expected for approach and avoid feedback such that approach feedback will be associated with positive emotions and avoid feedback will be associated with negative emotions. Now one need be careful not to conflate the feedback itself with the emotional outcomes that are downstream from such feedback. As noted, approach and avoid feedback do not *necessarily* have any inherent emotional valence, but it appears that there is likely a pattern for the downstream effects of approach and avoid feedback relevant to emotion.

Notably, these metanalyses have indicated that gain and loss frames themselves are not always predictive of persuasion (O'Keefe & Jensen, 2006), an important factor in media feedback. That is, media feedback is designed to be inherently persuasive to keep an individual in the loop or system. As such, Nabi and colleagues (2019) point out the importance of understanding the underlying mechanisms of gain and loss frames. This chapter takes a similar approach such that it hopes to see which variables are most important when examining approach and avoid feedback.

METHOD

For this chapter, a 2 (approach feedback, avoid feedback) x 2 (feedback indicating accurate response, feedback indicating inaccurate response) factorial experiment was employed to explore approach and avoid feedback in media. From there, participants were asked to fill out a questionnaire detailing their attitudes and perceptions specific to their condition.

All participants were asked to use a "new" online tool that allowed them to select stocks to hypothetically buy or sell, then the tool assessed the users' selections. This tool was based on existing stock watchlist media available on a number of websites. Notably, the tool was completely fabricated by the researcher to experimentally control for any confounding variables.

Participants in the approach feedback condition were told, "You can buy up to 100 shares of each of these stocks. Please choose your configuration that will maximize gains and the site will tell you how well you performed. *Please note that this tool is only used for this study and should not be used to inform your purchase or sale of stocks." Participants in the avoid feedback condition were told, "You can sell up to 100 shares of each of these stocks. Please choose your configuration that will minimize loss and the site will tell you how well you performed. *Please note that this tool is only used for this study and should not be used to inform your purchase or sale of stocks."

Those in the feedback indicating accurate response condition made their selections and then were told, "Your choices maximized and approached gain" or "Your choices minimized and avoided loss," depending on whether they were in the approach or avoid condition. Those in the feedback indicating inaccurate response condition made their selections then were told, "Your choices were not close to values that would increase gain. Please try again knowing that your goal is to approach the optimal threshold of gain" or "Your choices were too close to values that would increase loss. Please try again knowing that your goal is to minimize and avoid loss," depending on whether they were in the approach or avoid condition.

Measures

Each of the measures listed indicated acceptable reliability (competence α = .91, autonomy α = .84, relatedness α = .93, surveillance α = .93, information comprehensibility α = .75, information comprehensiveness α = .94, cognitive load α = .80). For information accuracy, the item, "The information in the tool is not precise" was removed and the remaining two items were correlated, r = .76, p < .01. Likewise, for relevance, the item, "The information in the tool does not help me at all" was removed and the remaining two items were correlated, r = .80, p < .01. Participants were also asked how often they looked at the stock market, consumed media about the stock market, and bought or sold stocks.

Participants

After removing participants who failed the attention checks, 275 remained. The participants were majority white (66.5%) females (53.1%) in their mid-30s (M = 35.67), and 54.9% made $59,999 or less. The sample also spent 2.74 days a week looking at the stock market, 2.41 hours per day consuming media about the stock market, and 1.56 days a week buying or selling stocks.

RESULTS

Feelings of enjoyment, discouragement, encouragement, entertainment, meaningfulness, competence, autonomy, relatedness, information accuracy, cognitive load, surveillance, information comprehensibility, information comprehensiveness, and information relevance were entered as dependent variables. The conditions were used as the independent variables. Age, gender, race, income, days a week looking at the stock market, days a week buying or selling stocks, and how often media about the stock market is consumed were entered as covariates. This analysis revealed a multivariate effect of approach/

avoid feedback ($F(14, 115) = 1.86$, $p < .05$, Wilks' $\Lambda = .81$, $\eta_p2 = .18$) but no effects of feedback indicating accuracy/inaccuracy nor were there any interaction effects.

The individual ANOVAs related to approach feedback and avoid feedback significantly impacted feelings of enjoyment ($F(1, 138) = 7.36$, $p < .01$, $\eta_p2 = .05$, Approach $M = 5.04$, $SD = 1.70$, Avoid $M = 4.46$, $SD = 1.65$), entertainment ($F(1, 138) = 4.64$ $p < .05$, $\eta_p2 = .03$, Approach $M = 4.60$, $SD = 1.81$, Avoid $M = 4.13$, $SD = 1.90$), competence ($F(1, 138) = 11.99$, $p < .001$, $\eta_p2 = .09$, Approach $M = 5.09$, $SD = 1.50$, Avoid $M = 4.32$, $SD = 1.61$), autonomy ($F(1, 138) = 3.92$, $p < .05$, $\eta_p2 = .03$, Approach $M = 4.91$, $SD = 1.55$, Avoid $M = 4.57$, $SD = 1.44$), information accuracy ($F(1, 138) = 7.91$, $p < .01$, $\eta_p2 = .06$, Approach $M = 4.60$, $SD = 1.47$, Avoid $M = 4.11$, $SD = 1.52$), cognitive load ($F(1, 138) = 3.85$, $p = .05$, $\eta_p2 = .03$, Approach $M = 2.84$, $SD = 1.47$, Avoid $M = 3.31$, $SD = 1.24$), information comprehensiveness ($F(1, 138) = 3.82$, $p = .05$, $\eta_p2 = .03$, Approach $M = 4.53$, $SD = 1.67$, Avoid $M = 4.08$, $SD = 1.76$), and relevance ($F(1, 138) = 5.50$, $p < .05$, $\eta_p2 = .04$, Approach $M = 4.90$, $SD = 1.37$, Avoid $M = 4.39$, $SD = 1.68$).

In order to fully test mediation, the PROCESS macro (Hayes, 2018) was used. Competence, autonomy, information accuracy, cognitive load, information comprehensiveness, and relevance were entered as mediators. Enjoyment was entered as the outcome variable. Approach or avoid feedback was entered as the independent variable. Age, gender, race, income, days a week looking at the stock market, days a week buying or selling stocks, and how often media about the stock market is consumed were entered as covariates. Model 4 using 2,000 bootstrap samples and 95 percent CI, was employed. The direct effect of the condition dissipated and there were no indirect effects for individual variables but an aggregate effect of all mediators.

When entertainment was entered as the outcome, the direct effect of the condition dissipated but there were indirect effects on enjoyment via competence (point estimate = -.21, Boot SE = .11, CI [-.45, -.03.]) and information accuracy (point estimate = -.24, Boot SE = .12, CI [-.52, -.03]).

Lastly, the previously prescribed hierarchical regression was used to examine the variables. In step 1, age, gender, race, income, days a week looking at the stock market, days a week buying or selling stocks, and how often media about the stock market is consumed were entered. In step 2, feelings of discouragement, encouragement, competence, autonomy, relatedness, information accuracy, cognitive load, surveillance, information comprehensibility, information comprehensiveness, and information relevance were entered. In step 3, the conditions were entered. Enjoyment was entered as the dependent variable. These results are detailed in table 3.1. This was run twice more with meaningfulness entered as the dependent variable and entertainment entered as the dependent variable (table 3.2 and 3.3).

Table 3.1 Regression Analysis for Enjoyment

	B	SE	β
Step 1			
Gender	.41	.30	.12
Age	-.02	.12	-.12
Race	.02	.08	.02
Income	-.03	.04	-.07
Looking at stocks	.28	.09	.35[b]
Days buying/selling stocks	-.06	.12	-.06
Consume media about stocks	.04	.06	.07
	$F_{(7, 138)} = 3.00$[b]		
	Adj. R^2 = .09		
Step 2			
Gender	-.30	.20	-.08
Age	.01	.01	.04
Race	.00	.05	.00
Income	-.01	.03	-.02
Looking at stocks	-.01	.06	-.01
Days buying/selling stocks	-.01	.08	-.01
Consume media about stocks	.01	.04	.02
Discouraging	-.06	.07	-.07
Encouraging	.16	.07	.18[a]
Competence	.19	.10	.19[a]
Autonomy	.22	.10	.19[a]
Relatedness	.11	.10	.12
Cognitive Load	.06	.11	.05
Surveillance	.08	.11	.08
Information Accuracy	.38	.12	.33[c]
Information Comprehensibility	.17	.10	.14
Information Comprehensiveness	-.10	.12	-.11
Relevance	-.11	.11	-.10
	$F_{(11, 138)} = 13.54$[c]		
	Adj. R^2 = .62		
Step 3			
Gender	-.26	.20	-.08
Age	.01	.01	.05
Race	.00	.05	.00
Income	-.01	.03	-.01
Looking at stocks	.01	.06	.01
Days buying/selling stocks	-.03	.08	-.03
Consume media about stocks	.02	.04	.04
Discouraging	-.07	.07	-.08
Encouraging	.18	.07	.20[a]
Competence	.18	.09	.13[a]
Autonomy	.22	.10	.19[a]
Relatedness	.11	.10	.12
Cognitive Load	.07	.11	.06
Surveillance	.08	.11	.08

(Continued)

Table 3.1   Regression Analysis for Enjoyment (*Continued*)

	B	SE	β
Information Accuracy	.37	.12	.32[b]
Information Comprehensibility	.17	.10	.14
Information Comprehensiveness	-.12	.13	-.13
Relevance	-.10	.11	-.09
Accurate	.17	.19	.05
Approach/Avoid	-.24	.20	-.07
	$F_{(2, 138)} = 12.34$[c]		
	Adj. R^2 = .62		

[a]$p < 0.05$. [b]$p < 0.01$, [c]$p < 0.001$. No superscript $p > 0.05$

The most salient finding in this study is that approach and avoid feedback provided multivariate effects while feedback indicating accuracy did not. This provides evidence that approach and avoid feedback is conceptually distinct from feedback indicating accuracy. In this case, approach and avoid feedback was more important to users than indication of accuracy.

Often, media feedback is thought of in simplistic terms such that it is purely meant to indicate if a user has done something "right" or "wrong." In this study, whether or not a user got the answer "right" or "wrong" was insignificant in the analysis. On its face, this indicates that feedback is a much more complicated concept than it has been treated in the past. This example is particularly germane because of the confusion in the existing literature that surrounds positive and negative feedback. As chapter 1 details, positive and negative feedback have been conflated, so it is not clear whether it refers to the emotional valence of the feedback—"you did very well, keep up the good work" and "you did poorly, you should try harder next time" (Burrow & Rainone, 2017; Carnagey & Anderson, 2005; Connellan & Zemke, 1993; Deng et al., 2017; Hattie & Timperley, 2007; Reinecke, et al., 2012)—or the more traditional view of the direction in which the input is directed with regard to the discrepancy between the input value and the goal value (Ramaprasad, 1983; Carver & Scheier, 2001), which does not have inherent emotional valence. As argued previously, this study indicates that it is likely more fruitful to refer to feedback in terms of approach and avoid behaviors.

This study showed that when an approach media feedback mechanism was used, feelings of enjoyment, entertainment, competence, autonomy, information accuracy, information comprehensiveness, and relevance were all significantly greater than when an avoid media feedback mechanism was employed. Following the same trend cognitive load was significantly lower when an approach media feedback mechanism was used than an avoid media feedback mechanism. This suggests broadly that approach media feedback mechanisms confer an advantage over avoid media feedback mechanisms.

Table 3.2 Regression Analysis for Meaningfulness

	B	SE	β
Step 1			
Gender	.59	.32	.15
Age	-.02	.01	-.13
Race	.05	.08	.05
Income	-.07	.05	-.12
Looking at stocks	.33	.09	.36[b]
Days buying/selling stocks	-.15	.13	-.14
Consume media about stocks	.13	.07	.20
	$F_{(7, 138)} = 4.87$[c]		
	Adj. R^2 = .16		
Step 2			
Gender	-.13	.22	-.03
Age	.11	.01	.07
Race	.01	.05	.01
Income	-.05	.03	-.09
Looking at stocks	.06	.06	.06
Days buying/selling stocks	-.13	.08	-.12
Consume media about stocks	.07	.05	.11
Discouraging	.00	.07	.00
Encouraging	.34	.08	.34[c]
Competence	.01	.09	.01
Autonomy	.08	.10	.06
Relatedness	.20	.11	.19
Cognitive Load	-.02	.11	-.01
Surveillance	.16	.12	.14
Information Accuracy	.11	.12	.08
Information Comprehensibility	.20	.11	.14
Information Comprehensiveness	.07	.13	.06
Relevance	-.03	.12	-.02
	$F_{(11, 138)} = 16.21$[c]		
	Adj. R^2 = .66		
Step 3			
Gender	-.13	.22	-.03
Age	.01	.01	.06
Race`	.01	.06	.01
Income	-.05	.03	-.09
Looking at stocks	.06	.07	.06
Days buying/selling stocks	-.13	.09	-.11
Consume media about stocks	.07	.05	.11
Discouraging	-.01	.08	-.01
Encouraging	.34	.08	.34[c]
Competence	.00	.10	.00
Autonomy	.08	.10	.06
Relatedness	.20	.11	.19
Cognitive Load	-.01	.12	.00
Surveillance	.16	.12	.15
Information Accuracy	.10	.13	.08

(Continued)

Table 3.2 Regression Analysis for Meaningfulness (*Continued*)

	B	SE	β
Information Comprehensibility	.19	.11	.14
Information Comprehensiveness	-.08	.13	-.07
Relevance	-.04	.12	-.03
Accurate	-.10	.21	-.03
Approach/Avoid	-.03	.22	-.01
	$F(2, 1138) = 14.39^c$		
	Adj. $R^2 = .66$		

[a]$p < 0.05$. [b]$p < 0.01$, [c]$p < 0.001$. No superscript $p > 0.05$

The study here comports with Nabi and colleagues' (2019) metanalysis findings and thus offers a direct bridge between framing theory and approach/avoid media feedback.

As for the regression tables, it is noteworthy that the effect of the experimental manipulation went away within each regression. This helps paint a broader picture regarding which elements of feedback are important to people when they are using media in this context—as always, the specific context of an experiment should be carefully considered. Participants felt more enjoyment from the media feedback when they felt more encouraged, more competent, more autonomy, and that the information was accurate. Participants felt the feedback was more meaningful when they felt encouraged. Participants felt more entertained from the media feedback when they looked at stocks more often, felt encouraged, autonomous, and related to others.

Table 3.3   Regression Analysis for Entertainment

	B	SE	β
Step 1			
Gender	.52	.31	.14
Age	-.02	.01	.-13
Race	.06	.08	.06
Income	-.08	.05	-.14
Looking at stocks	.41	.09	.47[c]
Days buying/selling stocks	-.07	.12	-.07
Consume media about stocks	.02	.07	.03
	$F_{(7, 138)} = 5.74$[c]		
	Adj. R^2 = .19		
Step 2			
Gender	-.15	.21	-.04
Age	.00	.01	.03
Race	.05	.05	.05
Income	-.04	.03	-.07
Looking at stocks	.14	.06	.16[a]
Days buying/selling stocks	.00	.08	.00
Consume media about stocks	-.03	.04	-.04
Discouraging	.06	.07	.06
Encouraging	.23	.07	.24[b]
Competence	-.02	.09	-.02
Autonomy	.30	.10	.23[b]
Relatedness	.26	.10	.26[a]
Cognitive Load	.06	.11	.04
Surveillance	.07	.11	.07
Information Accuracy	.20	.12	.16
Information Comprehensibility	.01	.10	.00
Information Comprehensiveness	-.14	.13	-.13
Relevance	-.18	.11	-.15
	$F_{(11, 138)} = 16.08$[c]		
	Adj. R^2 = .66		
Step 3			
Gender	-.14	.21	-.04
Age	.00	.01	.03
Race`	.05	.05	.05
Income	-.04	.03	-.07
Looking at stocks	.15	.06	.17[a]
Days buying/selling stocks	-.01	.08	-.01
Consume media about stocks	-.02	.05	-.03
Discouraging	-.06	.07	-.07
Encouraging	.25	.08	.24[b]
Competence	-.02	.09	-.02
Autonomy	.29	.10	.23[b]
Relatedness	.26	.11	.25[a]
Cognitive Load	-.05	.12	-.04
Surveillance	.08	.12	.07
Information Accuracy	.20	.12	.15

(Continued)

Table 3.3 Regression Analysis for Entertainment (*Continued*)

	B	SE	β
Information Comprehensibility	.01	.10	.01
Information Comprehensiveness	-.15	.13	-.14
Relevance	.18	.11	.15
Accurate	.07	.20	.02
Approach/Avoid	-.15	.21	-.04
	$F(2, 1138) = 14.35^{c}$		
	Adj. $R^2 = .66$		

[a]$p < 0.05$. [b]$p < 0.01$, [c]$p < 0.001$. No superscript p > 0.05

Chapter 4

Positive and Negative Feedback

In the previous chapters, a distinction has been made between approach/ avoid feedback and positively/negatively valenced emotional feedback in an effort to clarify conflicting uses of the terms. To reiterate, one of the most common discrepancies found in feedback literature is the use of positive feedback and negative feedback such that positive and negative feedback have been defined in terms of task performance evaluation and the corresponding emotional valence therein (Burrow & Rainone, 2017; Carnagey & Anderson, 2005; Connellan & Zemke, 1993; Deng et al., 2017; Hattie & Timperley, 2007; Reinecke, et al., 2012)—and in the domain of media feedback, this is the dominant notion—but more traditionally, positive and negative feedback refers to the direction in which the input value and the goal value are communicated to the actor (Ramaprasad, 1983; Carver & Scheier, 2001). This chapter, in concert with the approach/avoid feedback chapter, aims to specifically show that there is a difference between these two conceptualizations, that they deserve their own tracks of study, and should be treated differently. This book suggests using the terms positively/negatively valenced emotional feedback, as the emotional outcome is an expected byproduct of feedback, and approach/avoid feedback instead in order to reduce the confusion.

Given this central premise, the literature on emotion and feedback is worth reviewing. Värlander (2008, p. 154) asserted that "in the context of feedback situations, emotions have a focal role." Another experiment showed that the presence of feedback and different types of feedback can impact emotions (Pekrun et al., 2014). In this case, feedback condition and achievement predicted test-related emotions such as hope, anger, anxiety, hopelessness, and shame.

In yet another study, participants were given a wearable device that told the wearer his or her heart rate (Costa, et al., 2016). When the device was manipulated to show the wearers a lower heart rate, this lowered the level of anxiety felt by the participants. This study is reminiscent of a seminal study by Valins (1966) where college men were shown pictures of women while also hearing a recording of what they thought was their own heartbeats. When the heartbeat recording was manipulated to go faster, the men stated that they were more attracted to the women in the pictures than when the women in the pictures were viewed alongside the recording of a slowed heartbeat. Valins gave prescient knowledge regarding how people might react to feedback provided from wearable technology, an older study that remains conceptually strong in the modern media environment.

In this new media environment, Burrow and Rainone (2017) argued that when a person received positively valenced emotional feedback on a social media site in the form of likes, that translated to greater feelings of self-esteem. In a study covering a similar topic area, when women placed high value on social media, their psychological well-being was often based on the valenced emotional feedback they received on social media platforms (Sabik, Falat, & Magagnos, 2019).

These findings are not altogether surprising. Generally, people enjoy praise, acknowledgement, and recognition in Western cultures. Idioms like "you catch more bees with honey than with vinegar" underscore this central idea that, after performing a task, a person would prefer to be patted on the head and told "good job" than rapped across the knuckles with a ruler, sent to the corner wearing a dunce cap, and told "you are not good enough."

In short, research shows that positively valenced emotional feedback can engender positive emotions and negatively valenced emotional feedback can engender negative emotions. Despite this intuitive function of valenced emotional feedback and the supporting evidence of the intuition, another study using open-ended responses suggested a more complex picture such that positively and negatively valenced emotional feedback can engender a mixture of positive and negative emotions (Fong, et al., 2018). The current text argues that this sentiment is likely most accurate and suggests that there are many more nuanced variables at play beyond positive and negative emotions, especially in media environments.

To date, studies have shown that media are capable of eliciting emotions from consumers (Grizzard, Tamborini, Lewis, Wang, & Prabhu, 2014; Hartmann, Toz, & Brandon, 2010; Oliver, 2008), and media feedback appears to be a particularly effective mechanism for doing so. As a result, the remainder of this chapter will detail a study on positively and negatively valenced emotional feedback.

METHOD

In this study, the researchers employed a 2 (positively valenced emotional feedback, negatively valenced emotional feedback) x 4 (number of incorrect answers) factorial experiment. Participants participated in an online quiz. They were asked a series of multiple-choice questions on popular culture such as, "What was Elton John's first US No 1 hit?" "What is Woody Harrelson's middle name?" and "Freddie Mercury died in which year?" These questions were selected because they were adequately challenging but not impossible, especially with multiple-choice answers. This allowed for a larger degree of variance in the number of incorrect answers that were collected. Based on performance, participants received 0 incorrect, 1 incorrect, 2 incorrect or 3 incorrect.

On top of this, participants were randomly assigned to receive positively valenced emotional feedback or negatively valenced emotional feedback. In the positive condition, participants were told, "You were close but incorrect. The answer is [insert relevant answer]. You can still do well on the quiz" if they were incorrect and, "Your answer was correct and you answered quickly. Keep up the good work" if their answer was correct. In the negative performance evaluation condition, participants were told, "Your answer was incorrect. The answer is [insert relevant answer]. You should think more carefully next time" if they were incorrect and "Your answer was correct but it took you longer than it should have to answer. Try harder next time" if their answer was correct. Consequently, the negative condition attempted to elicit negative emotions regardless of the answer while the positive performance evaluation condition attempted to elicit positive emotions regardless of the answer because the literature points to that as essential to positively and negatively valenced emotional feedback outcomes.

From there, participants were asked to fill out a questionnaire detailing their attitudes and perceptions specific to their condition.

Measures

Each measure had acceptable reliability (competence $\alpha = .93$, autonomy $\alpha = .84$, relatedness $\alpha = .95$, surveillance $\alpha = .92$, information comprehensibility $\alpha = .76$, information comprehensiveness $\alpha = .91$). For cognitive load, when "How successful were you in accomplishing what you were asked to do?" was removed, $\alpha = .82$. For information accuracy, when "The information is not precise" was removed, $r = .59$, $p < .01$. For relevance, when "The information does not help me at all" was removed, $r = .54$, $p < .01$. The sample was also asked about how often they participated in trivia/quizzes.

Participants

After removing participants who failed the attention checks, 375 remained. The participants were majority white (71.7%) females (55.2%) in their mid-30s (M = 37.50), and 54.0% made $59,999 or less. The sample also participated in trivia/quizzes an average of 14.8 times a month with a minimum of 0 and maximum of 1,000

RESULTS

Feelings of enjoyment, discouragement, encouragement, entertainment, meaningfulness, competence, autonomy, relatedness, information accuracy, cognitive load, surveillance, information comprehensibility, information comprehensiveness, and information relevance were entered as dependent variables. Positively/negatively valenced emotional feedback and number of incorrect answers were used as the independent variables. Age, gender, race, income, and time spent playing trivia were entered as covariates. This analysis revealed a multivariate effect of positively/negatively valenced emotional feedback ($F(14, 343)$ = 4.71, p < .001, Wilks' Λ = .84, η_p2 = .16) and number of incorrect answers ($F(42, 368)$ = 3.49, p < .001, Wilks' Λ = .67, η_p2 = .12) but no interaction effects.

According to the corresponding ANOVAs, positively/negatively valenced emotional feedback significantly impacted feelings of enjoyment ($F(1, 368)$ = 20.09, p < .001, η_p2 = .05), entertainment ($F(1, 368)$ = 10.50, p < .01, η_p2 = .03), discouragement ($F(1, 368)$ = 24.41, p < .001, η_p2 = .06), encouragement ($F(1, 368)$ = 5.02, p < .05, η_p2 = .01), competence ($F(1, 368)$ = 6.75, p < .05, η_p2 = .01), autonomy ($F(1, 368)$ = 17.55, p < .001, η_p2 = .05), cognitive load ($F(1, 368)$ = 21.93, p < .001, η_p2 = .06),), and relevance ($F(1, 368)$ = 11.36, p < .05, η_p2 = .01), while number of incorrect answers significantly impacted feelings of enjoyment ($F(3, 368)$ = 11.85, p < .001, η_p2 = .09), entertainment ($F(3, 368)$ = 8.11, p < .001, η_p2 = .06), meaningfulness ($F(3, 368)$ = 12.31, pv< .001, η_p2 = .09), encouragement ($F(3, 368)$ = 8.72, p < .001, η_p2 = .07), competence ($F(3, 368)$ = 36.43, p < .001, η_p2 = .23), autonomy ($F(3, 368)$ = 4.38, p < .01, η_p2 = .04), relatedness ($F(3, 368)$ = 12.36, p < .001, η_p2 = .09), cognitive load ($F(3, 368)$ = 5.84, p < .001, η_p2 = .05),), surveillance ($F(3, 368)$ = 9.82, p < .001, η_p2 = .08), information accuracy ($F(3, 368)$ = 7.06, p < .001, η_p2 = .06), and relevance ($F(3, 368)$ = 6.15, p < .001, η_p2 = .05).

For positively/negatively valenced emotional feedback feelings of enjoyment (positive M = 5.20, SD = 1.60, negative M = 4.01, SD = 2.03), entertainment (positive M = 5.18, SD = 1.70, negative M = 4.28, SD = 2.02), discouragement (positive M = 2.94, SD = 1.92, negative M = 4.19, SD = 2.05), encouragement (positive M = 3.96, SD = 1.96, negative M = 3.14, SD = 2.00), competence (positive M = 4.15, SD = 1.81, negative M = 3.56, SD = 1.83), autonomy (positive M = 4.78, SD = 1.39, negative M = 4.00, SD = 1.55), cognitive load (positive M = 2.98, SD = 1.51, negative M = 3.76, SD = 1.31), and relevance (positive M = 5.01, SD = 1.43, negative M = 4.44, SD = 1.55) all provided results following intuition.

Positively valenced emotional feedback led to greater feelings of enjoyment, entertainment, encouragement, feelings of competence, autonomy, and feelings of relevance while positively valenced emotional feedback led to lower feelings of cognitive load and discouragement. These findings primarily comport with previous studies such that positively valenced emotional feedback will be more enjoyable and entertaining while providing feelings of competence, encouragement, and less discouragement as one would be more likely to think "I can do this." Generally, people also want to be associated with things that are positive, thus positively valenced emotional feedback was more relevant. The constant positivity also seemed to produce a lessened cognitive burden for the participants as performance was deemed acceptable even though the task was identical.

For number of incorrect answers, according to Bonferroni correction, there were a number of significant differences at $p < .05$. Results are summarized in table 4.1. Feelings of enjoyment, entertainment, encouragement, competence, relatedness, and relevance indicated that those who were incorrect on 0 and 1 question were significantly different than those who were incorrect on 2 and 3 questions. Differences for feelings of meaningfulness were primarily driven by those who were correct on all three and the other conditions as well as those who were incorrect on all three and the other conditions. For feelings of autonomy, the only differences were between those who were correct on all questions and those who missed two answers as well as those who answered one incorrectly and three incorrectly. Significant differences for cognitive

Table 4.1 Summary of means and standard deviations for significant differences between dependent variables for number of incorrect answers

Dependent Variable	0 Incorrect	1 Incorrect	2 Incorrect	3 Incorrect
Enjoyment	5.71, 1.21[a]	5.10, 1.68[a]	4.42, 1.92[b]	4.17, 1.95[b]
Entertainment	5.61, 1.10[a]	5.20, 1.62[a]	4.58. 1.98[b]	4.34, 2.08[b]
Encouragement	4.79, 1.63[a]	3.88, 1.90[a]	3.31, 2.07[b]	3.23, 1.90[b]
Competence	5.45, 1.00[a]	4.82, 1.45[a]	3.44, 1.72[b]	3.13, 1.84[b]
Relatedness	4.46,1.90[a]	3.56,1.92[a]	2.76,1.90[b]	2.71, 1.81[b]
Relevance	5.35, 1.23[a]	5.06, 1.47[a]	4.55, 1.50[b]	4.52, 1.55[b]
Meaningfulness	5.29, 1.00[a]	3.96, 2.02[b]	3.43, 2.02[bc]	3.25, 1.99[c]
Autonomy	4.96, 1.24[a]	4.59, 1.32[a]	4.19, 1.68[b]	4.28, 1.51[a]
Cognitive Load	4.13, 1.37[a]	3.54, 1.41[ab]	3.26, 1.47[bc]	3.06, 1.44[bc]
Surveillance	4.59, 1.64[a]	3.51, 1.78[b]	2.95, 1.76[b]	3.08, 1.75[b]
Information Accuracy	5.28, 1.02[ab]	5.35, 1.19[ab]	4.85, 1.29[ac]	4.66, 1.29[c]

According to Bonferroni correction, those that do not share a superscript differ at $p < .05$ or less. If they share a superscript, they were not significantly different.

load were between those who were correct on all answers and those who missed two or three answers. Differences in feelings of information accuracy were primarily driven by those who were incorrect on all questions and those who were incorrect on 0 and 1. There was also a significant difference between those who had one and two answers incorrect.

In all participants tended to feel more pleasant emotions and more informed when they answered more questions accurately. Again, this is not surprising. When comparing these findings to the approach/avoid feedback chapter, the number of answers correct resulted in more significant results than the incorrect/correct manipulation of the approach/avoid feedback chapter. Unto itself, this suggests that the way accuracy is communicated has a bearing on user reaction.

In order to fully test mediation, the PROCESS macro (Hayes, 2018) was used. Competence, autonomy, relatedness, information accuracy, cognitive load, encouragement, discouragement, and relevance were entered as mediators. Enjoyment was entered as the outcome variable. The positively/negatively valenced emotional feedback and number of incorrect answers were entered as the independent variables. Age, gender, race, income, and time spent playing trivia were entered as covariates. Model 8 using 2,000 bootstrap samples and 95 percent CI was employed. There were no direct effects of the conditions nor interaction effects. There were indirect effects on enjoyment via competence when participants had one answer incorrect (point estimate = -.10, Boot SE = .05, CI [-.23, -.02]) or two answers incorrect (point estimate = -.09, Boot SE = .05, CI [-.19, -.01]). There were indirect effects on enjoyment via autonomy when participants had one answer incorrect (point estimate = -.18, Boot SE = .07, CI [-.33, -.07]), two answers incorrect (point estimate = -.21, Boot SE = .06, CI [-.34, -.09]), or three answers incorrect (point estimate = -.24, Boot SE = .08, CI [-.42, -.09]). There were indirect effects on enjoyment via relevance when individual got two answers incorrect (point estimate = -.20, Boot SE = .07, CI [-.38, -.10.]) or three answers incorrect (point estimate = -.22, Boot SE = .11, CI [-.53, -.09]). There were indirect effects on enjoyment via discouragement when participants had one answer incorrect (point estimate = -.22, Boot SE = .08, CI [-.41, -.09]), two answers incorrect (point estimate = -.22, Boot SE = .07, CI [-.38, -.10.]), or three answers incorrect (point estimate = -.22, Boot SE = .08, CI [-.41, -.04]). There were indirect effects on enjoyment via encouragement when participants had one answer incorrect (point estimate = -.10, Boot SE = .05, CI [-.22, -.01.]), two answers incorrect (point estimate = -.13, Boot SE = .06, CI [-.26, -.03.]), or three answers incorrect (point estimate = -.17, Boot SE = .08, CI [-.40, -.04]).

The same procedure was replicated with meaningfulness entered as the outcome variable, and there were no direct effects of the conditions nor interaction effects. There were indirect effects on meaningfulness via relatedness when an individual had two answers incorrect (point estimate = -.10, Boot SE = .06, CI [-.23, -.01.]) or three answers incorrect (point estimate = -.15,

Boot SE = .08, CI [-.35, -.10]). There were indirect effects on meaningfulness via relevance when an individual had two answers incorrect (point estimate = -.07, Boot SE = .06, CI [-.30, -.06.]) or three answers incorrect (point estimate = -.24, Boot SE = .09, CI [-.43, -.07]). There were indirect effects on meaningfulness via encouragement when an individual had one answer incorrect (point estimate = -.22, Boot SE = .10, CI [-.45, -.03.]), two answers incorrect (point estimate = -.31, Boot SE = .09, CI [-.50, -.14]) or three answers incorrect (point estimate = -.39, Boot SE = .13, CI [-.67, -.16]).

The same procedure was replicated a third time with entertainment entered as the outcome variable and there were no direct effects of the conditions nor interaction effects. There were indirect effects on entertainment via autonomy when individuals had one answer incorrect (point estimate = -.16, Boot SE = .07, CI [-.31, -.05.]), two answers incorrect (point estimate = -.19, Boot SE = .07, CI [-.33, -.07]), or three answers incorrect (point estimate = -.21, Boot SE = .08, CI [-.41, -.07]). There were indirect effects on entertainment via relevance when individuals had two answers incorrect (point estimate = -.24, Boot SE = .08, CI [-.41, -.09]), or three answers incorrect (point estimate = -.35, Boot SE = .12, CI [-.60, -.13]). There were indirect effects on meaningfulness via discouragement when individuals had one answer incorrect (point estimate = -.17, Boot SE = .07, CI [-.34, -.05]), two answers incorrect (point estimate = -.17, Boot SE = .07, CI [-.32, -.06]), or three answers incorrect (point estimate = -.17, Boot SE = .09, CI [-.35, -.05]). There were indirect effects on meaningfulness via encouragement when individuals had one answer incorrect (point estimate = -.13, Boot SE = .07, CI [-.28, -.02.]), two answers incorrect (point estimate = -.18, Boot SE = .07, CI [-.33, -.06]), or three answers incorrect (point estimate = -.22, Boot SE = .09, CI [-.44, -.07]).

This is where significant differences can be found between the study on approach/avoid feedback and this study on positively/negatively valenced emotional feedback. There were only indirect effects on enjoyment via competence and information accuracy and no effects on entertainment in the previous study. While the manipulation (i.e., the type of media feedback used) is certainly part of the explanation for this, there are likely other factors and might be part of a larger picture accommodating for these disparate findings.

The prescribed hierarchical regression was used as a subsequent analysis. In step 1, age, gender, race, income, and time spent playing trivia were entered. In step 2, feelings of discouragement, encouragement, competence, autonomy, relatedness, information accuracy, cognitive load, surveillance, information comprehensibility, information comprehensiveness, and information relevance were entered. In step 3, the conditions were entered. Enjoyment was entered as the dependent variable. These results are detailed in Table 4.2. This was run twice more with meaningfulness entered as the dependent variable and entertainment entered as the dependent variable (table 4.3 and table 4.4).

Table 4.2 Regression Analysis for Enjoyment

	B	SE	β
Step 1			
Gender	-.40	.20	-.10[a]
Age	.01	.01	.07
Race	-.08	.06	-.08
Income	-.04	.03	-.06
Play Trivia	.00	.00	.06
	$F(5, 368) = 2.27$[a]		
	Adj. $R^2 = .02$		
Step 2			
Gender	-.16	.13	-.04
Age	.00	.00	.00
Race	-.07	.04	-.06
Income	-.01	.02	-.02
Play Trivia	.00	.00	.03
Discouraging	-.19	.04	-.21[c]
Encouraging	.19	.05	.20[c]
Competence	.18	.05	.17[b]
Autonomy	.26	.06	.21[c]
Relatedness	.06	.06	.06
Cognitive Load	.01	.08	.01
Surveillance	-.01	.07	.01
Information Accuracy	-.01	.08	-.01
Information Comprehensibility	.22	.08	.14[b]
Information Comprehensiveness	.02	.08	.02
Relevance	.30	.07	.24[c]
	$F(11, 368) = 32.75$[c]		
	Adj. $R^2 = .58$		
Step 3			
Gender	-.16	.13	-.04
Age	.00	.00	.01
Race	-.07	.04	-.06
Income	-.01	.02	-.02
Play Trivia	.00	.00	.03
Discouraging	-.18	.04	-.19[c]
Encouraging	.18	.05	.19[c]
Competence	.15	.05	.15[b]
Autonomy	.25	.06	.20[c]
Relatedness	.06	.06	.07
Cognitive Load	.03	.07	.02
Surveillance	-.01	.07	-.01
Information Accuracy	-.02	.08	-.01
Information Comprehensibility	.24	.08	.15[b]
Information Comprehensiveness	.02	.08	.02
Relevance	.29	.07	.23[c]
#Incorrect	-.10	.08	-.05
Positive/Negative	-.31	.14	-.08[a]
	$F(2, 368) = 29.82$[c]		
	Adj. $R^2 = .58$		

[a] $p < 0.05$. [b] $p < 0.01$, [c] $p < 0.001$. No superscript $p > 0.05$.

Table 4.3 Regression Analysis for Meaningfulness

	B	SE	β
Step 1			
Gender	-.64	.21	-.16[b]
Age	.00	.01	-.03
Race`	-.10	.06	-.09
Income	-.08	.03	-.13[b]
Play Trivia	.00	.00	.04
	$F(5, 368) = 3.94$[b]		
	Adj. $R^2 = .04$		
Step 2			
Gender	-.10	.13	-.02
Age	.01	.01	.05
Race`	-.04	.04	-.03
Income	-.02	.02	-.04
Play Trivia	.00	.00	-.01
Discouraging	-.07	.04	-.08
Encouraging	.34	.05	.33[c]
Competence	.12	.05	.11[a]
Autonomy	-.07	.06	-.05
Relatedness	.17	.06	.16[b]
Cognitive Load	.09	.07	.06
Surveillance	.18	.07	.16[b]
Information Accuracy	.00	.08	.00
Information Comprehensibility	-.04	.08	-.03
Information Comprehensiveness	.09	.08	.06
Relevance	.24	.07	.18[c]
	$F(11, 368) = 39.48$[c]		
	Adj. $R^2 = .63$		
Step 3			
Gender	-.10	.13	-.02
Age	.01	.01	.05
Race`	-.04	.04	-.03
Income	-.02	.02	-.04
Play Trivia	.00	.00	-.01
Discouraging	-.08	.04	-.08
Encouraging	.35	.05	.34[c]
Competence	.11	.05	.10[a]
Autonomy	-.05	.06	-.04
Relatedness	.17	.06	.16[b]
Cognitive Load	.06	.07	.04
Surveillance	.19	.07	.16
Information Accuracy	-.01	.08	.00
Information Comprehensibility	-.05	.08	-.03
Information Comprehensiveness	.09	.08	.06
Relevance	.24	.07	.18[c]
#Incorrect	-.05	.08	-.02
Positive/Negative	.16	.15	.04
	$F(2, 368) = 35.14$[c]		
	Adj. $R^2 = .62$		

[a]$p < 0.05$. [b]$p < 0.01$, [c]$p < 0.001$. No superscript $p > 0.05$.

Table 4.4   Regression Analysis for Entertainment

	B	SE	β
Step 1			
Gender	-.16	.20	-.04
Age	.01	.01	.09
Race`	-.08	.06	-.07
Income	-.05	.03	-.08
Play Trivia	.00	.00	.03
	$F(5, 368) = 1.85$		
	Adj. $R^2 = .01$		
Step 2			
Gender	.08	.14	.02
Age	.01	.01	.05
Race`	-.06	.04	-.05
Income	-.03	.02	-.04
Play Trivia	.00	.00	.00
Discouraging	-.14	.04	-.15[b]
Encouraging	.22	.05	.23[c]
Competence	.12	.05	.12[a]
Autonomy	.22	.06	.17[c]
Relatedness	.04	.07	.04
Cognitive Load	.01	.07	.01
Surveillance	.02	.07	.02
Information Accuracy	-.04	.08	-.03
Information Comprehensibility	.19	.09	.12[a]
Information Comprehensiveness	.01	.08	.12
Relevance	.36	.07	.29[c]
	$F(11, 368) = 25.81^c$		
	Adj. $R^2 = .52$		
Step 3			
Gender	.08	.14	.02
Age	.01	.01	.05
Race`	-.06	.04	-.06
Income	-.03	.02	-.05
Play Trivia	.00	.00	.00
Discouraging	-.14	.04	-.15[b]
Encouraging	.22	.05	.23[c]
Competence	.10	.06	.10
Autonomy	.22	.06	.17[c]
Relatedness	.04	.07	.04
Cognitive Load	.00	.07	.00
Surveillance	.02	.07	.02
Information Accuracy	-.05	.08	-.03
Information Comprehensibility	.19	.09	.12[a]
Information Comprehensiveness	.02	.08	.01
Relevance	.36	.07	.28[c]
#Incorrect	-.07	.08	-.04
Positive/Negative	-.03	.16	-.01
	$F(2, 368) = 22.91^c$		
	Adj. $R^2 = .52$		

[a]$p < 0.05$. [b]$p < 0.01$, [c]$p < 0.001$. No superscript $p > 0.05$.

For the regression tables, note that the effects of the experimental manipulation went away by the last step. This suggests that too much may be made of positively and negatively valenced emotional feedback and performance itself. Participants felt more enjoyment from the media when they felt it was more relevant to them, when the information was comprehensible, when they felt competent and encouraged, but not when they felt discouraged. Participants felt the media was more meaningful when they felt it was more relevant to them, they felt related to others, competent, and encouraged. Participants felt more entertained from the media feedback when they felt it was more relevant to them, the information was comprehensible, they felt more autonomous, encouraged, and less discouraged.

In conjunction with the previous chapter, this study shows that performance itself and how performance is communicated to the user are important to media feedback loops. Regardless, there is a difference between positively/negatively valenced emotional feedback and approach/avoid feedback. When this distinction is made and understood, advancements to feedback literature will be more fruitful and useful in theory and in practice.

Chapter 5

Implicit versus Explicit
Media Feedback

As noted, there is a body of feedback literature dedicated specifically to implicit and explicit feedback. This is a fairly prominent area in media feedback literature that merits attention and clear conceptualization. Implicit feedback is a loop that is not clear and direct, as opposed to explicit feedback. For example, a user can give a platform implicit feedback through behaviors on that platform like clicks and time spent on a page. Meanwhile, a user can give explicit feedback through comment forms and posts made to the platform support page. Likewise, users can receive implicit feedback through suggestions or cues on a platform and explicit feedback through directives from the platform.

To date, much of the academic attention has focused on implicit feedback. "Types of implicit feedback include purchase history, browsing history, search patterns, or even mouse movements. For example, a user that purchased many books by the same author probably likes that author" (Hu et al., 2008, p. 1). When providing feedback "recommenders can infer user preferences from . . . implicit feedback" which "indirectly reflect(s) opinion through observing user behavior" (Hu, Koren, & Volinsky, 2008; Oard, & Kim, 1998). Much of this literature comes from the perspective of the feedback provider and how to interpret user behaviors to effectively provide feedback (Joachims et al., 2017; Rendle et al., 2012). Consequently, more understanding is needed on how implicit feedback impacts users.

Despite such clear-cut conceptualizations from extant literature, critical differences in media environments complicate the topic. Different media platform configurations must be considered wherein the users receive implicit feedback and/or explicit feedback. For example, if someone clicks on an unavailable option while using a software program, the computer might make an audible tone indicating that the option is not available. Likewise, if an

47

option is unavailable, the button may be grayed out, subtly indicating that the user cannot click on the button at this point, as opposed to explicit feedback which would denote a clear error on the user end through text or a pop-up window telling the user that the option is not available.

Clear examples can be found in Juul's (2010) description of the video game *Guitar Hero* as effective video game feedback, virtually all of it implicit to the user.

> In *Guitar Hero*, when players are performing well, a recognizable song plays, the screen lights up with bonuses, and the crowd cheers with delight. When players are performing poorly, harsh, out-of-tune notes interrupt the song, the screen changes to an ominous color, and the crowd boos the performance. But *Guitar Hero* only represents one example of video game feedback. Even older games, like *Pac-Man*, use feedback. Each ghost Pac-Man eats shows a point value, which is then added to the player's total score. On top of the visual satisfaction of seeing the score increase, the game uses audio cues to denote certain behaviors. Pac-Man's iconic "wakka wakka" indicates the game is still going and points are still being accrued. Alternately, the player hears a lowering droop when Pac-Man dies, indicating a setback to the game goal. It is no coincidence that *Pac-Man* and *Guitar Hero* were wildly popular when they were first released (Rogers, 2016).

Implicit media feedback can include visuals or aural cues like a flash or a chime or even a rumble from a game controller (Ahn, 2011; Lim et al., 2012; Wood, Griffiths, Chappell, & Davies, 2004). This is opposed to explicit feedback which tells the user directly that he or she is doing well or poorly. The purpose of this chapter is to test the difference between these two types of media feedback.

METHOD

For this study, a 2-condition experiment addressed the impact of implicit and explicit media feedback. Participants were randomly assigned to a condition. Participants read through an interactive story adapted from Rogers, Dillman-Carpentier, and Barnard (2016).

> The featured story follows the actions of a captured spy who is being held at an enemy stronghold, likely facing execution. In an escape attempt, the spy pries a ventilation cover loose, crawls through the ducts into a hallway, and eventually enters a room where he/she is spotted by the enemy (p.35-36).

At the end of the story, the character escapes. The story is told in second person (you) to create a feeling of immersion and also to emulate Choose Your

Own Adventure books as well as text-based adventure video games and video games broadly. The story was told in segments and after each segment the participants were able to make a choice about the action they (the character) took in the story.

In the implicit feedback condition, participants were told, "A color flash indicates a correct or incorrect decision." Based on established protocols from video games and from American culture broadly, red and green were selected where green was meant to represent a positive outcome and red was meant to represent a negative outcome.

In the explicit feedback condition, participants were told, "You will be told if you make the correct or incorrect decision." After each choice, participants were told, "You made the wrong decision" or "You made the right decision."

In order to experimentally control for what content was encountered and the valence of the feedback, the feedback presented was the same for each participant. The first two choices were met with "You made the wrong decision" or a red flash. The next two decisions were met with "You made the right decision" or a green flash. Regardless of the choices made by the participants, they always proceeded in the game/story. From there, participants were asked to fill out a questionnaire detailing their attitudes and perceptions specific to their condition.

MEASURES

Each of the measures indicated acceptable reliability (competence $\alpha = .92$, autonomy $\alpha = .85$, relatedness $\alpha = .94$, surveillance $\alpha = .92$, cognitive load $\alpha = .70$, information comprehensibility $\alpha = .68$, information comprehensiveness $\alpha = .89$). For information accuracy, the item, "The information is not precise" was removed and the remaining two items were correlated, $r = .68$, $p < .01$. For relevance, the item, "The information does not help me at all." was removed and the remaining two items were correlated, $r = .68$, $p < .01$. The sample was also asked how often they read fiction, Choose Your Own Adventure stories, and spy stories.

PARTICIPANTS

After removing participants who failed the attention checks, 178 remained. The participants were majority white (74.7%) females (53.4%) in their late-30s ($M = 39.30$), and 57.3% made $59,999 or less. The sample also read fiction on average of 7.74 ($SD = 10.01$) hours per week, read Choose Your Own

Adventure stories for 2.29 (*SD* = 6.74) hours per week, and read spy stories for 1.72 (*SD* = 4.48) hours per week.

RESULTS

Feelings of enjoyment, discouragement, encouragement, entertainment, meaningfulness, competence, autonomy, relatedness, information accuracy, cognitive load, surveillance, information comprehensibility, information comprehensiveness, and information relevance were entered as dependent variables. The implicit and explicit feedback condition was used as the independent variable. Age, gender, race, income, time spent reading, time spent reading Choose Your Own Adventure stories, and time spent reading spy stories were entered as covariates. This analysis revealed a multivariate effect of implicit and explicit feedback that did not approach significance ($F(15, 155)$ = .57, p = .89, Wilks' Λ = .95, η_p^2 = .05).

The lack of findings here indicated that, from an end-user perspective, there is no difference between explicit media feedback and implicit media feedback. Perhaps in the current media landscape, where people are constantly surrounded by feedback, frequently using devices, they have become more media literate, and implicit feedback has become more noticeable, more evident to the user. Indeed, some people are able to identify the computer-generated sounds when an email arrives versus the sound when a new message on Discord arrives without an explicit pop-up or directive from the computer. People may have become so accustomed to subtle forms of feedback in media that the distinction between implicit and explicit feedback has blurred—this assumes that there was a difference between implicit and explicit media feedback for the end user in the first place. This is relevant because much of the literature discussed comes from a content creation viewpoint. There are clear differences regarding means of production for implicit and explicit feedback, but these differences may not be as important to users as previously thought. Perhaps software and hardware designers have become so adept at designing implicit feedback for users, end users may not notice much of a difference between explicit and implicit media feedback.

Another possibility is that users *never* made such a clear distinction between implicit and explicit feedback. Consider the following example: in a classroom if a student answers a question incorrectly and the teacher tells the student that he or she is wrong how different will the student's perception be than if the teacher simply made a face indicating that the answer was incorrect? The difference may be negligible to the student even though the types of feedback are categorically different based on the implicit/explicit dichotomy.

The same could be true of media. If someone playing a video game or using a piece of software receives an explicit error message, it may have the same impact on the user than if the screen flashed red.

One more possibility, and perhaps the most likely, is that the manipulation in this experiment was too weak to garner significant results.

Given the lack of results, the PROCESS macro was not used but the prescribed hierarchical regression was used. In step 1, age, gender, race, income, how often participants read, how often participants read Choose Your Own Adventure stories, and how often participants read spy stories were entered. In step 2, feelings of discouragement, encouragement, competence, autonomy, relatedness, information accuracy, cognitive load, surveillance, information comprehensibility, information comprehensiveness, and information relevance were entered. In step 3, the condition was entered. Enjoyment was entered as the dependent variable. These results are detailed in table 5.1. This was run twice more with meaningfulness entered as the dependent variable and entertainment entered as the dependent variable (table 5.2 and 5.3).

In the model for enjoyment, higher feelings of encouragement and relevance but lesser feelings of surveillance predicted more enjoyment. The negative relationship with surveillance is interesting. Perhaps since the story requires a degree of suspension of disbelief and escape from reality, one might expect that surveillance would have a deleterious effect on enjoyment.

In the model for feelings of meaningfulness, gender (female), and greater feelings of encouragement, competence, and information comprehensiveness, as well as lesser feelings of information comprehensibility predicted greater feelings of meaningfulness. Women connected more with the story and the story was more meaningful when one felt encouragement and competence. The findings related to information comprehensiveness and information comprehensibility merit further discussion. These findings give some indication that implicit feedback and explicit feedback may be different despite the lack of findings in this chapter. When feedback was comprehensive it was more meaningful and when feedback was less comprehensible, there were greater feelings of meaningfulness. These traits can be tied to implicit and explicit feedback. One would assume that more information comprehensiveness would be found in explicit feedback, but less information comprehensibility would be found in implicit feedback. Perhaps there are times when explicit or implicit feedback would be preferred and other times when it does not matter to the user. Likewise, participants might view implicit feedback as comprehensive in this story and more explicit feedback might have pulled participants out of the story. Regardless, this should be treated as conjecture given the lack of findings from the experimental manipulation.

In the model for entertainment, whiteness, greater perceptions of encouragement, feedback frequency, autonomy, and relevance as well as lesser

Table 5.1   Regression Analysis for Enjoyment

	B	SE	β
Step 1			
Gender	.03	.24	.10
Age	.01	.01	.10
Race	-.07	.06	-.08
Income	.01	.04	.03
Time reading	.01	.02	.09
Reading CYOA stories	.00	.03	.02
Reading spy stories	.01	.04	.04
	$F_{(7, 170)} = 1.07$		
	Adj. R^2 = .00		
Step 2			
Gender	.21	.18	.07
Age	.01	.01	.05
Race	-.02	.05	-.02
Income	.00	.03	-.01
Time reading	.00	.01	.00
Reading CYOA stories	-.01	.02	-.04
Reading spy stories	.02	.03	.05
Discouraging	-.05	.06	-.06
Encouraging	.30	.06	.33[c]
Frequency	.01	.07	.01
Competence	.13	.08	.11
Autonomy	.28	.09	.24[b]
Relatedness	-.04	.07	-.05
Cognitive Load	-.09	.10	-.06
Surveillance	-.18	.09	-.20[a]
Information Accuracy	.00	.11	.00
Information Comprehensibility	-.06	.13	-.04
Information Comprehensiveness	.17	.12	.13
Relevance	.43	.10	.35[c]
	$F_{(12, 170)} = 10.42^c$		
	Adj. R^2 = .50		
Step 3			
Gender	.21	.18	.07
Age	.00	.01	.04
Race	-.02	.05	-.03
Income	-.01	.03	-.02
Time reading	.00	.01	.01
Reading CYOA stories	-.01	.02	-.04
Reading spy stories	.02	.03	.06
Discouraging	-.06	.06	-.06
Encouraging	.30	.06	.33[c]
Frequency	.01	.07	.01
Competence	.13	.08	.11
Autonomy	.28	.09	.25[b]
Relatedness	-.03	.07	-.04
Cognitive Load	-.09	.10	-.07

(Continued)

Table 5.1   Regression Analysis for Enjoyment (*Continued*)

	B	SE	β
Surveillance	-.18	.09	-.20[a]
Information Accuracy	-.01	.11	-.01
Information Comprehensibility	-.07	.13	-.04
Information Comprehensiveness	.19	.12	.14
Relevance	.44	.10	.36[c]
Condition	.29	.17	.09
	$F(1, 170) = 10.14$[c]		
	Adj. $R^2 = .51$		

[a]$p < 0.05$. [b]$p < 0.01$, [c]$p < 0.001$. No superscript $p > 0.05$.

perceptions of surveillance led to greater feelings of entertainment. In the case of this story, entertainment was multifaceted and associated with a number of generally positive outcomes. The surveillance argument for the enjoyment model can likely be replicated here. The feedback frequency finding is unique. Frequency is regarded as an important piece of a feedback loop.

Most importantly, this chapter provided no evidence of differences between implicit and explicit feedback for the user. This finding should not be overstated but rather interpreted as one iteration of implicit and explicit feedback. Indeed, this should be a call for more attention to this area as there is more to unpack with this type of media feedback.

Table 5.2   Regression Analysis for Meaningfulness

	B	SE	β
Step 1			
Gender	.45	.27	.12
Age	-.01	.01	-.11
Race	-.01	.07	-.01
Income	-.05	.04	-.08
Time reading	-.02	.02	-.09
Reading CYOA stories	.08	.03	.27[a]
Reading spy stories	.05	.04	.13
	$F(7, 170) = 3.79$[b]		
	Adj. $R^2 = .10$		
Step 2			
Gender	.45	.20	.12[a]
Age	.00	.01	.01
Race	.01	.05	.01
Income	-.05	.03	-.09
Time reading	-.01	.02	-.04
Reading CYOA stories	.02	.02	.07
Reading spy stories	.01	.03	.04
Discouraging	-.12	.07	-.12
Encouraging	.31	.07	.30[c]
Frequency	.06	.08	.04
Competence	.19	.09	.15[a]
Autonomy	.03	.10	.02
Relatedness	.13	.07	.13
Cognitive Load	-.02	.11	-.02
Surveillance	.12	.09	.12
Information Accuracy	.17	.12	.11
Information Comprehensibility	-.47	.14	-.26[b]
Information Comprehensiveness	.29	.13	.19[a]
Relevance	.08	.11	.06
	$F(12, 170) = 13.54$[c]		
	Adj. $R^2 = .57$		
Step 3			
Gender	.45	.20	.12[a]
Age	.00	.01	.01
Race`	.01	.05	.01
Income	-.05	.03	-.09
Time reading	-.01	.02	-.04
Reading CYOA stories	.02	.02	.06
Reading spy stories	.01	.03	.03
Discouraging	-.12	.07	-.12
Encouraging	.31	.07	.30[c]
Frequency	.06	.08	.04
Competence	.19	.09	.15[a]
Autonomy	.03	.10	.02
Relatedness	.13	.07	.13
Cognitive Load	.02	.11	.01

(Continued)

Table 5.2   Regression Analysis for Meaningfulness (*Continued*)

	B	SE	β
Surveillance	.12	.09	.12
Information Accuracy	.17	.12	.12
Information Comprehensibility	-.46	.14	-.25[b]
Information Comprehensiveness	.29	.13	.19[a]
Relevance	.08	.11	.06
Condition	-.08	.19	-.02
	F(7, 170) = 12.80[c]		
	Adj. R^2 = .57		

[a]$p < 0.05$. [b]$p < 0.01$, [c]$p < 0.001$. No superscript $p > 0.05$.

Table 5.3   Regression Analysis for Entertainment

	B	SE	β
Step 1			
Gender	.09	.25	.03
Age	.00	.01	.03
Race	-.17	.06	-.20[a]
Income	.01	.04	.01
Time reading	.01	.02	.08
Reading CYOA stories	.02	.03	.08
Reading spy stories	-.02	.04	-.05
	$F(7, 170) = 1.74$		
	Adj. $R^2 = .03$		
Step 2			
Gender	.26	.19	.08
Age	.00	.01	-.03
Race	-.13	.05	-.15[a]
Income	-.01	.03	-.03
Time reading	.00	.01	.01
Reading CYOA stories	.01	.02	.04
Reading spy stories	-.02	.03	-.06
Discouraging	.06	.06	.07
Encouraging	.31	.07	.34[c]
Frequency	.16	.07	.14[a]
Competence	.12	.08	.11
Autonomy	.28	.10	.24[b]
Relatedness	-.01	.07	-.01
Cognitive Load	-.04	.11	-.03
Surveillance	-.29	.09	-.32[c]
Information Accuracy	.05	.11	.04
Information Comprehensibility	-.21	.14	-.13
Information Comprehensiveness	.17	.13	.12
Relevance	.39	.10	.31[c]
	$F(12, 170) = 10.24$[c]		
	Adj. $R^2 = .50$		
Step 3			
Gender	.26	.19	.08
Age	.00	.01	-.03
Race	-.13	.05	-.15[b]
Income	-.01	.03	-.03
Time reading	.00	.01	.01
Reading CYOA stories	.01	.02	.04
Reading spy stories	-.02	.03	-.06
Discouraging	-.06	.06	-.07
Encouraging	.31	.07	.34[c]
Frequency	.16	.08	.14[a]
Competence	.12	.08	.11
Autonomy	.28	.09	.24[b]
Relatedness	-.01	.07	-.01
Cognitive Load	-.11	.09	-.11

(Continued)

Table 5.3 Regression Analysis for Entertainment (*Continued*)

	B	SE	β
Surveillance	-.29	.09	-.32[c]
Information Accuracy	.05	.11	.04
Information Comprehensibility	-.21	.14	-.13
Information Comprehensiveness	.17	.13	.13
Relevance	.39	.10	.32[c]
Condition	.08	.18	.02
	$F(1, 170) = 9.68$[c]		
	Adj. $R^2 = .49$		

[a]$p < 0.05$. [b]$p < 0.01$, [c]$p < 0.001$. No superscript $p > 0.05$.

Chapter 6

Frequency of Media Feedback

The frequency of feedback is often noted as a key element to create effective feedback. When referring to feedback frequency, several terms are used regularly such as frequent, continuous, ongoing, informal, and real-time (Tseng et al., 2019). For the purpose of this chapter, frequency will be used. Frequency of feedback refers to *how often* a user receives information from the system. For example, the feedback system might provide information to the user once a day, every hour, every minute, etc.

Conventional wisdom has been that frequency of information in a feedback system is essential to any activity that requires more than one input. To use a mechanical example, if a train is using an automated feedback system regarding routes, delays, speed, safety, etc., a reasonable assumption would be that frequent, if not, continuous information would be preferable in order to maintain the most efficient and safe train schedule. Without frequent information, safety and efficiency could be compromised. In a human example, frequent information performs similarly. Consider the industry of personal athletic trainers. This industry exists because people desire more frequent information during exercise than they would receive in a class or working out on their own. People want to enter a system that provides more frequent information via the trainer. The person exercising can get constant information about appropriate weight use, body positioning and on which muscles an exercise should target.

This desire for constant information in a feedback system is perhaps best illustrated by the compulsive use of smartphones (Keefe, 2019). Driven by a need to fill in spaces of boredom or to receive information in a feedback system (texts, emails, playing games), people check their phones with great frequency. This has entered the public consciousness to the extent that it has led to a new term, nomophobia, which describes the fear of being without a

smartphone. One could argue that nomophobia is contiguous with the appre-
hension users feel when they are removed from a feedback system. That is,
if the smartphone is the platform for the feedback system, then lack of access
to the smartphone would remove the individual from the feedback system,
increasing negative emotional states.

Well-designed video games make use of frequent feedback (Rogers 2016).
In many video games, players navigate a virtual space. Inside this space, players know whether or not they are on-track based on information they receive
from the game's feedback system. The more often that information is delivered, the more "on-track" the player should be in accomplishing the tasks set
out by the game. If the information is not frequent, then the player is more
likely to get "lost" and not move toward game goals. Notably, some games
deliberately do this in order to encourage play and exploration. These games
are classified as sandbox games and are less focused on directional feedback
loops, but this is a deliberate decision by game designers.

In sum, frequency of feedback information is important because it helps
direct inputs more often, and this chapter experimentally tests the importance of this concept. To date, many researchers have asserted that frequent
feedback information confers advantages over less frequent feedback information. Wulf and colleagues (1998) argue that when someone is learning a
complex motor skill as opposed to a simple task, frequent feedback information leads to benefits up until a level of expertise is achieved. Similarly, in
another more recent study, Wulf and colleagues (2010) showed that when
feedback information was provided after every attempt on a task, participants
outperformed those receiving less frequent feedback. Notably, this was examining externally focused feedback, meaning the information was not about the
person but about the object upon which the person was acting. In a classroom
environment, frequent feedback information is critical to student development as well as the instructor's understanding of the student's development
(Bernstein & Allen, 2013). In a health context, more frequent feedback information was more useful in helping people reach their dietary and body weight
goals than when feedback information was less frequent (Celis-Morales et al.,
2019). This evidence suggests that frequent feedback information in media
environments would function in a similar capacity.

Despite all the evidence indicating that feedback should be frequent, frequent feedback has not always conferred benefits over less frequent feedback.
For example, frequent feedback can be maladaptive as it can interrupt necessary learning processes (Schmidt, 1991). Also, if feedback is unfavorable
and frequent, then it can have deleterious effects on effort and performance
as the individual is constantly reminded of how poorly he or she is doing
(Anand, Webb, & Wong, 2019). Wulf and colleagues (2010) offer a robust
review of literature that supports the notion that reduced feedback frequency

information has positive outcomes (e.g., Nicholson & Schmidt, 1991; Weeks & Kordus, 1998; Winstein & Schmidt, 1990; Wulf & Schmidt, 1989) and just as many studies do not offer the same conclusion (e.g., Dunham & Mueller, 1993; Sparrow, 1995; Sparrow & Summers, 1992; Wishart & Lee, 1997). As a result, this chapter aims to contribute to this conversation on feedback frequency within the specific domain of media feedback.

METHOD

For this study, a 2-condition experiment addressed the impact of feedback frequency. Participants were randomly assigned to a condition. Participants read through an interactive story adapted from Rogers, Dillman-Carpentier, and Barnard (2016)—the same story used in the implicit and explicit feedback chapter.

In the low frequency condition, participants proceeded through the story and by the end encountered the message "Great job! You made the correct decisions to escape." In the high frequency condition, participants proceeded through the story and were given feedback after each choice such as, "Good choice. You have made it to the next section," "That was a close one but you made it to the next section," "That was a tough call but you made the right one and live to continue the story," "Great choice! You are almost there!" and lastly, by the end, encountered the message "Great job! You made the correct decisions to escape." In order to experimentally control for what content was encountered and the valence of the feedback, there was no fail state. Regardless of the choices made by the participants, they always proceeded in the story.

From there, participants were asked to fill out a questionnaire detailing their attitudes and perceptions specific to their condition.

Measures

Each of the measures indicated acceptable reliability (competence $\alpha = .90$, autonomy $\alpha = .89$, relatedness $\alpha = .95$, surveillance $\alpha = .91$, cognitive load $\alpha = .82$, information comprehensibility $\alpha = .71$, information comprehensiveness $\alpha = .86$, relevance $\alpha = .70$). For information accuracy, the item, "The information is not precise" was removed and the remaining two items were correlated, $r = .76$, $p < .01$. For information comprehensibility, the item, "The information is not presented in an adequate way" was removed and the remaining three items were related, $\alpha = .90$. For relevance, the item, "The information does not help me at all" was removed and the remaining two items were correlated, $r = .60$, $p < .01$. The sample was also asked how often they read fiction, choose your own adventure stories, and spy stories.

Participants

After removing participants who failed the attention checks, 194 remained. The participants were majority white (68.0%) males (50.5%) in their mid-30s ($M = 37.43$), and 55.2% made $69,999 or less. The sample also read on average of 7.54 ($SD = 9.12$) hours per week, read choose your own adventure stories for 2.00 ($SD = 9.12$) hours per week, and read spy stories for 1.38 ($SD = 3.20$) hours per week.

RESULTS

Feelings of enjoyment, discouragement, encouragement, entertainment, meaningfulness, competence, autonomy, relatedness, information accuracy, cognitive load, surveillance, information comprehensibility, information comprehensiveness, and information relevance were entered as dependent variables. Feedback frequency was used as the independent variable. Age, gender, race, income, time spent reading, time spent reading choose your own adventure stories, and time spent reading spy stories were entered as covariates.

This analysis revealed a multivariate effect of feedback frequency that approached significance ($F(14, 165) = 1.72$, $p = .05$, Wilks' $\Lambda = .87$, $\eta_p2 = .13$). This echoes the literature detailed earlier. The literature, seemingly in nearly equal measure (Dunham & Mueller, 1993; Nicholson & Schmidt, 1991; Sparrow, 1995; Sparrow & Summers, 1992; Weeks & Kordus, 1998; Winstein & Schmidt, 1990; Wishart & Lee, 1997; Wulf et al., 2010; Wulf & Schmidt, 1989), is split on the importance of frequency of feedback information. Some of these studies argue that frequency is critical while others are unable to replicate those findings. The current chapter sits in between those two perspectives as the findings are on the threshold of significance.

Given these tenuous results, the PROCESS macro was not used and the prescribed hierarchical regression was employed. In step 1, age, gender, race, income, how often participants read, how often participants read choose your own adventure stories, and how often participants read spy stories were entered. In step 2, feelings of discouragement, encouragement, competence, autonomy, relatedness, information accuracy, cognitive load, surveillance, information comprehensibility, information comprehensiveness, and information relevance were entered. In step 3, the feedback frequency was entered. Enjoyment was entered as the dependent variable. These results are detailed in table 6.1. This was run twice more with meaningfulness entered as the dependent variable and entertainment entered as the dependent variable (table 6.2 and 6.3).

Table 6.1 Regression Analysis for Enjoyment

	B	SE	β
Step 1			
Gender	-.09	.18	-.04
Age	.00	.01	-.03
Race	.05	.05	.07
Income	-.02	.03	-.05
Time reading	-.01	.01	-.05
Reading CYOA stories	.01	.03	.03
Reading spy stories	.04	.04	.09
	$F(7, 191) = .65$		
	Adj. $R^2 = .01$		
Step 2			
Gender	.03	.14	.01
Age	.00	.01	-.01
Race	.01	.04	.01
Income	-.02	.02	-.05
Time reading	.01	.01	.04
Reading CYOA stories	-.01	.02	-.04
Reading spy stories	.00	.03	.00
Discouraging	-.06	.06	-.08
Encouraging	.27	.05	.35[c]
Frequency	-.02	.06	-.02
Competence	.03	.08	.02
Autonomy	.23	.07	.22[b]
Relatedness	.01	.06	.02
Cognitive Load	-.01	.08	-.01
Surveillance	.00	.07	.00
Information Accuracy	-.06	.08	-.06
Information Comprehensibility	-.01	.10	-.01
Information Comprehensiveness	.18	.10	.16
Relevance	.29	.09	.25[b]
	$F(12, 191) = 8.44$[c]		
	Adj. $R^2 = .42$		
Step 3			
Gender	.01	.14	.01
Age	.00	.01	-.02
Race	.00	.04	.00
Income	-.02	.02	-.05
Time reading	.01	.01	.04
Reading CYOA stories	-.01	.02	-.04
Reading spy stories	.00	.03	.00
Discouraging	-.07	.05	-.10
Encouraging	.27	.05	.34[c]
Frequency	.00	.07	.00
Competence	.02	.08	.02
Autonomy	.24	.07	.23[b]
Relatedness	-.02	.07	-.03

(Continued)

Table 6.1 **Regression Analysis for Enjoyment (*Continued*)**

	B	SE	β
Cognitive Load	.00	.08	.00
Surveillance	.00	.07	.00
Information Accuracy	-.06	.08	-.06
Information Comprehensibility	.00	.10	.00
Information Comprehensiveness	.18	.10	.16
Relevance	.29	.09	.24[b]
Condition	-.22	.15	-.09
	$F(1, 191) = 8.18$[c]		
	Adj. $R^2 = .43$		

[a]$p < 0.05$. [b]$p < 0.01$, [c]$p < 0.001$. No superscript $p > 0.05$.

For the results of the regressions, enjoyment was impacted by encourage-ment, autonomy, and relevance. When interacting with a choose your own adventure story/text-based adventure game, these items were pathways to enjoyment. Feelings of meaningfulness were predicted by feelings of encour-agement, relatedness, and surveillance. Entertainment was predicted by feel-ings of encouragement and relevance.

While this chapter does not shine much light on the issue of feedback fre-quency, it does provide more data on media feedback—in this case, choose your own adventure story and text-based adventure games. The results regarding frequency mirror the literature on the frequency of feedback infor-mation. In some cases, the importance of frequency may be overstated or perhaps frequency is more salient in specific situations. Another possibility is that the manipulation was not strong enough or the experiment required another condition. Nevertheless, more research on the importance of feed-back frequency is needed as there is not a clear answer here or in the existing literature.

Table 6.2   Regression Analysis for Meaningfulness

	B	SE	β
Step 1			
Gender	-.50	.24	-.14[a]
Age	.00	.01	-.03
Race	.14	.07	.14
Income	-.03	.04	-.05
Time reading	-.04	.02	-.20[a]
Reading CYOA stories	.08	.03	.20[a]
Reading spy stories	.05	.05	.08
	$F(7, 191) = 3.70$[b]		
	Adj. $R^2 = .09$		
Step 2			
Gender	-.25	.19	-.07
Age	.00	.01	-.01
Race	.02	.06	.02
Income	.00	.03	.00
Time reading	.01	.01	.03
Reading CYOA stories	-.01	.03	-.02
Reading spy stories	-.05	.04	-.08
Discouraging	.01	.08	.01
Encouraging	.30	.07	.27[c]
Frequency	.00	.09	.00
Competence	.16	.11	.09
Autonomy	.01	.10	.01
Relatedness	.28	.08	.27[c]
Cognitive Load	.00	.11	.00
Surveillance	.30	.09	.27[b]
Information Accuracy	-.09	.11	-.06
Information Comprehensibility	-.16	.14	-.09
Information Comprehensiveness	.16	.13	.10
Relevance	.17	.12	.10
	$F(12, 191) = 10.95$[c]		
	Adj. $R^2 = .50$		
Step 3			
Gender	-.20	.19	-.07
Age	.00	.01	-.02
Race	.02	.06	.02
Income	.00	.03	.00
Time reading	.01	.01	.03
Reading CYOA stories	-.01	.02	-.04
Reading spy stories	-.05	.04	-.09
Discouraging	.01	.09	.01
Encouraging	.30	.07	.27[c]
Frequency	.00	.09	.00
Competence	.16	.11	.09
Autonomy	.01	.10	.01
Relatedness	.28	.08	.27[c]

(Continued)

Table 6.2   Regression Analysis for Meaningfulness (*Continued*)

	B	SE	β
Cognitive Load	.00	.11	.00
Surveillance	.30	.09	.27[b]
Information Accuracy	-.09	.11	-.06
Information Comprehensibility	-.16	.14	-.09
Information Comprehensiveness	.16	.13	.10
Relevance	.17	.12	.10
Condition	-.05	.20	-.01
	$F(1, 191) = 10.35^{c}$		
	Adj. $R^2 = .49$		

[a]$p < 0.05$. [b]$p < 0.01$, [c]$p < 0.001$. No superscript $p > 0.05$.

Table 6.3   Regression Analysis for Entertainment

	B	SE	β
Step 1			
Gender	-.09	.18	-.04
Age	.00	.01	-.03
Race	.03	.05	.05
Income	-.02	.03	-.06
Time reading	-.01	.01	-.05
Reading CYOA stories	-.01	.03	-.03
Reading spy stories	.03	.04	.09
	$F(7, 191) = .42$		
	Adj. $R^2 = .02$		
Step 2			
Gender	.00	.15	.00
Age	.00	.01	-.01
Race	.02	.04	.04
Income	-.02	.02	-.06
Time reading	.01	.01	.05
Reading CYOA stories	-.02	.02	-.09
Reading spy stories	.01	.03	.03
Discouraging	-.04	.06	-.05
Encouraging	.20	.06	.25[b]
Frequency	.06	.07	.06
Competence	.17	.09	.14
Autonomy	.13	.08	.13
Relatedness	.06	.06	.09
Cognitive Load	-.13	.09	-.13
Surveillance	-.04	.07	-.05
Information Accuracy	-.02	.09	-.02
Information Comprehensibility	-.02	.11	-.02
Information Comprehensiveness	.09	.10	.08
Relevance	.29	.10	.24[b]
	$F(12, 191) = 6.55$[c]		
	Adj. $R^2 = .36$		
Step 3			
Gender	-.02	.15	-.01
Age	.00	.01	-.02
Race	.02	.04	.03
Income	-.02	.02	-.06
Time reading	.01	.01	.05
Reading CYOA stories	-.02	.02	-.08
Reading spy stories	.01	.03	.02
Discouraging	-.05	.06	-.07
Encouraging	.19	.06	.24[b]
Frequency	.09	.07	.09
Competence	.16	.09	.14
Autonomy	.14	.08	.14
Relatedness	.06	.06	.08

(Continued)

Table 6.3   Regression Analysis for Entertainment (*Continued*)

	B	SE	β
Cognitive Load	-.11	.09	-.11
Surveillance	-.04	.07	-.05
Information Accuracy	-.02	.09	-.02
Information Comprehensibility	-.01	.11	-.01
Information Comprehensiveness	.09	.10	.08
Relevance	.29	.10	.24[b]
Condition	-.24	.16	-.09
	$F(1, 191) = 6.38^c$		
	Adj. $R^2 = .36$		

[a]$p < 0.05$. [b]$p < 0.01$, [c]$p < 0.001$. No superscript $p > 0.05$.

Chapter 7

Timeliness of Media Feedback

Another characteristic that is widely accepted as critical to feedback effectiveness is timeliness.

Imagine a classroom full of students. These students have just taken a mid-term exam that is worth half of their final grade. Half of the students immediately receive their graded exams from the instructor while the other half are told that they will have to wait several weeks for their grades. From a practical perspective, the students who receive their grades have a distinct advantage over those who do not. Those who receive their grades receive an assessment on their performance and can calibrate their behavior in class to work toward success. The other students do not have this advantage. Psychologically, this would be distressing, raise anxiety, and perhaps even incite some students to anger. Those who received the feedback information on their exams would be less likely to experience these effects provided that they were pleased with their respective performances on the exam. In this example, the point is that people desire feedback information in a timely manner for both practical and psychological reasons.

This same example can be extended to media feedback information. If someone pushes a button on a remote to start a movie on a streaming service and the device does not respond promptly, the person might curse at the television and push the button again in frustration. When a person orders a product online and the confirmation email takes a day or two to arrive, that time without confirmation could produce feelings of anxiety and might prompt the person to contact customer service. A person may use his or her patient portal from his or her medical provider in order to get in touch with his or her doctor's office as it seems like a quick option. If the doctor's office responds quickly, the person will likely be satisfied but if not, the person will likely feel as if they are being deprived of otherwise timely feedback.

In fact, the current media landscape has likely increased people's desire for timely feedback information. Now that smartphones and instantaneous message delivery are normalized, people can contact one another at virtually any time in seconds provided the infrastructure is in place.

When feedback is not timely, it creates the feeling that subject matter is "distant and remote" (Higgins, Hartley, & Skelton, 2002, p. 55; MacKenzie, 1974) or discouraging (Vrasidas & McIsaac, 1999). Perceptions of interactivity also decrease as the feedback process is delayed (Barboza & da Silva, 2016). Mediated classroom environments rely on timeliness in the feedback process otherwise feedback is not effective (Eom, Wen, & Ashill, 2006). Higgins and colleagues add "timely feedback is vital" (p. 62) and a timely feedback process is essential to the efficacy of feedback (Poulos & Mahony, 2008). In other words, feedback must be timely to work effectively.

Nicol (2010) provides a definition of feedback timeliness such that feedback is timely if it is sent before the next related task is performed—note that this definition indicates a process, not one piece of information. In other words, for example, people playing a video game need to know if they made the right or wrong move in the game before they try again. Notably, there is empirical evidence that there is a threshold for timeliness such that, at a certain point, feedback is considered timely regardless of how quickly is delivered (Bayerlein, 2014); when feedback is considered fast, making it faster will not impact user perceptions. The Nicol definition is useful and needs to be considered within the broader context of the feedback loop. For example, people who post on Instagram may expect feedback more quickly while people playing online chess asynchronously may expect feedback more slowly.

There is a plethora of studies indicating the importance of timeliness in feedback. Most of these studies are done within the context of education such that timely feedback refers to instructors providing timely assessments to students. The fact that most of this literature comes from the education discipline is not an issue, as conceptually, the notions discussed can easily be transferred to media. In fact, some of these educational studies mentioned discuss timely feedback specifically within the context of online teaching which could be considered media feedback. When reading these studies the notion of feedback just needs to be understood as a process not as simply information.

In summary, there is a large degree of evidence that timely feedback confers advantages over slower feedback. However, there is a ceiling effect where the effect of the speed of the feedback begins to diminish.

METHOD

This study employed a 3-condition experiment to address the impact of timeliness in feedback. From there, participants were asked to fill out a questionnaire detailing their attitudes and perceptions specific to their condition.

All participants were told, "Pretend you are the editor of an online website. You must select a photo for the cover of your website. The photos have all been ranked by professional photographers as effective for the website or ineffective for the website. Please do your best to select an effective photograph as determined by professional photographers." Beneath this text was five photographs for the participant to choose from. Those in condition 1 were told "Your feedback should be instantaneous" and the feedback information was made available one second after selection. Those in condition 2 were told "Your feedback may take up to 30 seconds to generate." and the feedback information was made available 30 seconds after selection. Those in condition 3 were told "Your feedback may take up to 60 seconds to generate" and the feedback information was made available 60 seconds after selection.

Regardless of their selection, participants were told, "Congratulations! You have selected an effective photograph as determined by the professional photographers." Notably, the photographs were not ranked by professional photographers as the study was experimentally controlling for the type of feedback information received.

Measures

Each of the measures indicated acceptable reliability (competence $\alpha = .94$, autonomy $\alpha = .89$, relatedness $\alpha = .92$, surveillance $\alpha = .95$, cognitive load $\alpha = .87$, information comprehensibility $\alpha = .73$, information comprehensiveness $\alpha = .91$,). For information accuracy, the item, "The information in the tool is not precise" was removed and the remaining two items were correlated, $r = .76$, $p < .001$. Likewise, for relevance, the item, "The information in the tool does not help me at all" was removed and the remaining two items were correlated, $r = .69$, $p < .001$. Participants were also asked to rank their own expertise in photography.

Participants

After removing participants who failed the attention checks, 282 remained. The participants were majority white (72.1%) females (50.5%) in their mid-30s ($M = 37.04$), and 58.4 percent made $69,999 or less. The sample also considered themselves an average of 3.63 ($SD = 1.73$) on a scale of 1–7 as experts in photography.

RESULTS

Feelings of enjoyment, discouragement, encouragement, entertainment, meaningfulness, competence, autonomy, relatedness, information accuracy, cognitive load, surveillance, information comprehensibility, information comprehensiveness, and information relevance were entered as dependent variables. Timeliness in feedback was used as the independent variable. Age, gender, race, income, and expertise in photography were entered as covariates. This analysis revealed no multivariate effect of feedback information timeliness and none of individual ANOVAs related to feedback information timeliness were significant.

The manipulation appears to not have worked so the prescribed hierarchical regression was used. In step 1, age, gender, race, income, and photography expertise were entered. In step 2, feelings of discouragement, encouragement, competence, autonomy, relatedness, information accuracy, cognitive load, surveillance, information comprehensibility, information comprehensiveness, and information relevance were entered. In step 3, the condition was entered. Enjoyment was entered as the dependent variable. These results are detailed in table 7.1. This was run twice more with meaningfulness entered as the dependent variable and entertainment entered as the dependent variable (table 7.2 and 7.3).

The most noteworthy finding here is the fact that timeliness of feedback information had no impact on any of the dependent variables despite a robust edifice of empirical studies suggesting otherwise (Barboza & da Silva, 2016; Eom, et al., 2006; Higgins, et al., 2002, p. 55; MacKenzie, 1974; Vrasidas & McIsaac, 1999). Exploring why this was the case is important given the contrary evidence.

Bayerlein (2014) indicated that feedback can be indistinguishable if it is all very timely. Perhaps this manipulation was not strong enough such that instant feedback information, feedback information delayed 30 seconds, and feedback information delayed 60 seconds were not different enough from one another to generate significant results. This may be particularly accurate if someone is taking a survey online and can simply browse another webpage while they wait for the allotted time to pass. Had the delay been much longer or if done in a lab, there may have been significant effects.

Another conjecture is that timeliness of feedback is only as important as the feedback is to the user. Take the example at the start of this chapter, the classroom full of students where half of the students received their graded exams from the instructor while the other half are told that they will have to wait several weeks for their grades. For an engaged and invested student, this would likely make a considerable difference both in performance of the student and psychological state of the student. On the other hand, for a

Table 7.1 Regression Analysis for Enjoyment

	B	SE	β
Step 1			
Gender	.35	.16	.13[a]
Age	.00	.00	-.01
Race`	-.03	.04	-.05
Income	.02	.02	.05
Photography expertise	.14	.05	.19[b]
	$F(5, 263) = 2.52$[a]		
	Adj. $R^2 = .02$		
Step 2			
Gender	.22	.12	.08
Age	.00	.00	.06
Race`	-.04	.03	-.05
Income	-.01	.02	-.02
Photography expertise	.00	.04	.00
Discouraging	-.12	.04	-.17[c]
Encouraging	.10	.04	.13[a]
Competence	.14	.07	.13[a]
Autonomy	.27	.06	.26[c]
Relatedness	.06	.05	.06
Cognitive Load	.03	.06	.03
Surveillance	-.01	.05	-.02
Information Accuracy	.08	.07	.08
Information Comprehensibility	.17	.07	.15[b]
Information Comprehensiveness	-.02	.06	-.02
Relevance	.14	.07	.15[a]
	$F(11, 263) = 17.53$[c]		
	Adj. $R^2 = .49$		
Step 3			
Gender	.26	.12	.10[a]
Age	.00	.00	-.05
Race`	-.02	.03	-.03
Income	-.01	.02	-.03
Photography expertise	.00	.04	.00
Discouraging	-.14	.04	-.18[b]
Encouraging	.10	.04	.13[a]
Competence	.15	.07	.24[a]
Autonomy	.28	.06	.27[c]
Relatedness	.07	.05	.08
Cognitive Load	.06	.06	.06
Surveillance	-.01	.05	-.02
Information Accuracy	.09	.07	-.02
Information Comprehensibility	.19	.06	.17[b]
Information Comprehensiveness	-.02	.06	-.03
Relevance	.16	.07	.17[a]
Condition	-.17	.07	.10[a]
	$F(1, 263) = 17.11$[c]		
	Adj. $R^2 = .49$		

[a] $p < 0.05$. [b] $p < 0.01$, [c] $p < 0.001$. No superscript $p > 0.05$.

Table 7.2 Regression Analysis for Meaningfulness

	B	SE	β
Step 1			
Gender	.08	.20	.02
Age	.00	.01	.03
Race`	-.02	.05	-.02
Income	-.04	.03	-.08
Photography expertise	.37	.06	.37[c]
	$F(5, 263) = 9.46^c$		
	Adj. $R^2 = .13$		
Step 2			
Gender	.06	.15	.02
Age	.01	.01	.06
Race`	.00	.04	.00
Income	-.04	.02	-.08
Photography expertise	.07	.05	.07
Discouraging	-.05	.06	-.05
Encouraging	.22	.05	.22[c]
Competence	.05	.08	.04
Autonomy	.12	.08	.08
Relatedness	.12	.07	.11
Cognitive Load	-.03	.08	-.03
Surveillance	.27	.06	.31[c]
Information Accuracy	.08	.09	.06
Information Comprehensibility	-.04	.08	-.03
Information Comprehensiveness	.06	.08	.05
Relevance	.19	.09	.12
	$F(11, 263) = 20.89^c$		
	Adj. $R^2 = .53$		
Step 3			
Gender	.08	.15	.02
Age	.01	.01	.06
Race`	.01	.04	.01
Income	-.04	.02	-.08
Photography expertise	.07	.05	.07
Discouraging	-.05	.06	-.06
Encouraging	.22	.06	.22[a]
Competence	.05	.09	.03
Autonomy	.12	.08	.09
Relatedness	.12	.07	.11
Cognitive Load	-.03	.08	-.03
Surveillance	.27	.06	.30[c]
Information Accuracy	.08	.09	.06
Information Comprehensibility	-.04	.08	-.03
Information Comprehensiveness	.05	.08	.05
Relevance	.16	.09	.12
Condition	-.07	.09	-.03
	$F(1, 263) = 19.67^c$		
	Adj. $R^2 = .53$		

[a]$p < 0.05$. [b]$p < 0.01$, [c]$p < 0.001$. No superscript $p > 0.05$.

Table 7.3 Regression Analysis for Entertainment

	B	SE	β
Step 1			
Gender	.08	.17	.03
Age	.00	.01	-.01
Race`	-.07	.05	-.08
Income	.01	.03	.03
Photography expertise	.12	.05	.15[a]
	$F(5, 263) = 1.57$		
	Adj. R^2 = .01		
Step 2			
Gender	-.06	.14	-.02
Age	.00	.01	-.02
Race`	.07	.04	.09
Income	.00	.02	.02
Photography expertise	-.05	.05	-.06
Discouraging	-.03	.05	-.04
Encouraging	.19	.05	.22[c]
Competence	.11	.08	.10
Autonomy	.02	.07	.01
Relatedness	.19	.06	.19[b]
Cognitive Load	-.07	.07	-.07
Surveillance	.11	.05	.15[a]
Information Accuracy	-.09	.08	-.08
Information Comprehensibility	.18	.08	.14[a]
Information Comprehensiveness	.07	.07	.08
Relevance	.16	.08	.16[a]
	$F(11, 263) = 14.08$[c]		
	Adj. R^2 = .43		
Step 3			
Gender	-.03	.14	-.02
Age	.00	.01	-.01
Race`	-.06	.03	-.07
Income	.00	.02	.01
Photography expertise	-.05	.05	-.06
Discouraging	-.03	.05	-.04
Encouraging	.19	.05	.22[c]
Competence	.10	.08	.09
Autonomy	.02	.07	.02
Relatedness	.19	.06	.19[b]
Cognitive Load	-.07	.07	-.07
Surveillance	.11	.05	.15
Information Accuracy	-.08	.08	-.08
Information Comprehensibility	.18	.08	.14[a]
Information Comprehensiveness	.07	.07	.08
Relevance	.17	.08	.16[a]
Condition	-.11	.08	-.07
	$F(1, 263) = 13.11$[c]		
	Adj. R^2 = .43		

[a] $p < 0.05$. [b] $p < 0.01$, [c] $p < 0.001$. No superscript $p > 0.05$.

disengaged student who is not invested in his or her grades, timeliness would likely make no difference in performance of the student nor the psychological state of the student. The disengaged student does not care about the feedback information; therefore, the feedback received is irrelevant and does not matter when it is received. A disengaged student may not even notice how long it takes for feedback information to be delivered. For example, a disengaged student may not even notice when grades are posted online while a more engaged student would check for the postings often. In this experimental manipulation, participants were not likely invested in the selection of the photograph because they had no investment in the hypothetical website. The likelihood that the photograph choice was relevant was quite low.

This explanation can be extended to media feedback. If someone pushes a button on a remote to change the channel and it does not respond, the person may not curse at the television and push the button in frustration. Instead, the person might be absent-mindedly channel surfing, so the lack of timely feedback is irrelevant. When a person orders a product online and the confirmation email takes a day to show up, that time may not produce feelings of anxiety and might not prompt the person to contact customer service because the person might have ordered something mundane like bulk toothpaste. For the people using their patient portal in order to get in touch with their doctor's office, they might not want an answer right away in case it contains bad news, or they may not feel the information is all that important.

As a result, the evidence from this chapter suggests that timeliness, on its face, is not as important as stated in previous research. The individual receiving the feedback must be invested in the feedback as a precursor. The feedback must be relevant to him or her in order for timeliness to matter in a feedback loop.

As for the regression tables, feedback information was most enjoyable when the participant was female, it was less discouraging, more encouraging, engendered feelings of competence and autonomy, the information was comprehensible, and relevant. Interestingly and despite the lack of findings using multivariate analysis, the condition showed that people enjoyed the feedback information more when it was timelier. This shows some support for the previous research. Indeed, the position of this book is not that timeliness is irrelevant in feedback loops, only that timeliness likely has precursor requirements. Note that relevance was also a significant part of this model lending credence to the notion that feedback must be relevant for timeliness to be impactful. Beyond that, one can surmise that women enjoy working with photographs more than men and feeling more competent, autonomous, and encouraged is enjoyable.

Feedback information was found to be meaningful when it was encouraging and when it engendered feelings of surveillance. Encouragement again, can create positive connections between people and platforms. Surveillance in this case, attaining information, predicted more meaningful experiences, perhaps because participants were getting information from a panel of experts, the information felt informative and led to deeper feelings of connection to others.

Finally, feedback information was entertaining when it was encouraging and relevant, also when it was more comprehensible and made participants feel related to others. This shows that there were a series of variables that were important for feedback. Encouragement was always a significant factor. Relevance was often a significant factor. Then, there also appeared to be feelings of connection developed between the users and the fake panel of photography experts. This is noteworthy as this suggests that who is providing the feedback can factor into user perceptions.

Chapter 8

Relevance of Media Feedback

In the chapter on timeliness and feedback, the argument was made that the effect of feedback timeliness is contingent upon the feedback's relevance to the user. This chapter examines that topic specifically. Relevance is another trait that should be inherent to effective feedback loops. A feedback loop should only be as effective as it is providing relevant information on relevant goals.

Relevance refers to the notion that something is closely connected to the individual. Within the domain of media feedback, this can be viewed in a variety of ways. First, the feedback itself can be relevant to the user regardless of the mechanics of the feedback loop. For example, an individual may care about the weather before entering a feedback loop regarding the weather. Or someone might be particularly invested in the stock market before entering a feedback loop regarding the stock market. In these cases, media feedback will be inherently relevant to the user ipso facto.

On the other hand, the feedback loop can become relevant or irrelevant to the user through its mechanisms. For example, if someone looks up information online about the weather and gets information on the stock market (as opposed to looking up information about the weather and getting information on the weather), that feedback is irrelevant as the user is not receiving feedback information that pertains to the feedback loop. The feedback loop creates irrelevance or relevance through the mechanisms it relies upon. The same is accurate, if someone looks up information online about the stock market and gets information on the weather. Another example of this would be if an individual selected a background for his or her computer only to find a different image was in its place. This type of relevance or irrelevance may not be inherent to the user, but it can be generated by the feedback loop. Given the lack of ability to fully control for inherent relevance and the conceptual

79

distinctions between the two, this chapter focuses on feedback loop generated relevance. This lack of matching in feedback loops can create a lack of
relevance for users. This can be frustrating to users and cause them to lose
interest quickly.

METHOD

For this study, a 2-condition experiment addressed the impact of media feedback relevance. Participants were randomly assigned to a condition (relevant
or non-relevant).

This study used a similar stimulus as the timeliness and feedback chapter. All participants were told, "Pretend you are the editor of an online
website. You must select a photo for the cover of your website. The photos have all been ranked by professional photographers as effective for
the website or ineffective for the website. Please do your best to select
an effective photograph as determined by professional photographers."
Beneath this were five photographs for the participants to choose from.
Those in condition 1, the relevance condition, selected a photograph. Then,
they were told "This was the photograph you selected," and the photograph
selected by the participants was displayed back to the participant. Beneath
that it read "Congratulations! You have selected an effective photograph
as determined by the professional photographers." Like with the timeliness
study, the photographs were not ranked by professional photographers as
the study was experimentally controlling for the type of feedback information received.

Those in condition 2, the non-relevant condition, selected a photograph.
Then, they were told "This was the photograph you selected," and a photograph they had not selected was displayed back to the participants, this was a
brand-new photograph that did not appear as an option for selection. Beneath
that it read "Congratulations! You have selected an effective photograph as
determined by the professional photographers." This was done to create a
lack of relevance generated by the feedback loop. In other words, the feedback loop helped in making the user feel like the loop was not relevant to
him or her.

From there, participants were asked to fill out a questionnaire detailing
their attitudes and perceptions specific to their condition.

Measures

Each of the measures indicated acceptable reliability (competence $\alpha = .93$,
autonomy $\alpha = .92$, relatedness $\alpha = .93$, surveillance $\alpha = .95$, cognitive load α

= .83, information comprehensibility α = .71, information comprehensiveness α = .92, relevance α =.70). For information accuracy, the item "The information in the tool is not precise" was removed and the remaining two items were correlated, r = .82, p < .01. Participants were also asked to rank their own expertise in photography.

Participants

After removing participants who failed the attention checks, 194 remained. The participants were majority white (69.6%) females (59.8%) in their mid-30s (M = 35.57), and 55.7 percent made $69,999 or less. The sample also considered themselves on average of 3.51 (SD = 1.76) on a scale of 1 – 7 as experts in photography.

RESULTS

Feelings of enjoyment, discouragement, encouragement, entertainment, meaningfulness, competence, autonomy, relatedness, information accuracy, cognitive load, surveillance, information comprehensibility, information comprehensiveness, and information relevance were entered as dependent variables. The condition (relevant vs non-relevant) was used as the independent variable. Age, gender, race, income, and expertise in photography were entered as covariates. This analysis revealed a multivariate effect of feedback relevance ($F(14, 165)$ = 2.71, p < .01, Wilks' Λ = .81, η_p^2 = .19).

The individual ANOVAs related to relevance significantly impacted feelings of enjoyment (($F(1, 178)$ = 4.91, p < .05, η_p^2 = .03), Relevant M = 5.93, SD = 1.33, Non-relevant M = 5.42, SD = 1.62), competence (($F(1, 178)$ = 8.90, p < .01, η_p^2 = .05), Relevant M = 5.62, SD = 1.23, Non-relevant M = 5.08, SD = 1.50), information accuracy (($F(1, 178)$ = 20.98, p < .001, η_p^2 = .10), Relevant M = 5.06, SD = 1.26, Non-relevant M = 4.09, SD = 1.84), information comprehensibility (($F(1, 178)$ = 5.00, p < .05, η_p^2 = .10), Relevant M = 5.51, SD = 1.11, Non-relevant M = 5.09, SD = 1.36), and relevance (($F(1, 178)$ = 7.46, p < .01, η_p^2 = .04), Relevant M = 5.36 SD = 1.28, Non-relevant M = 4.81 SD = 1.75).

In order to fully test mediation, the PROCESS macro (Hayes, 2018) was used.

Competence, information accuracy, information comprehensibility, and relevance were entered as mediators. Enjoyment was entered as the outcome variable. The condition was entered as the independent variable. Age, gender, race, income, and photography expertise were entered as covariates. Model 4 using 2,000 bootstrap samples and 95 percent CI, was employed. The direct effect of the condition dissipated but there were indirect effects on enjoyment via

competence (point estimate = -.28, Boot SE = .12, CI [-.57, -.08.]) and information comprehensibility (point estimate = -.10, Boot SE = .06, CI [-.23, -.01]).

First and foremost, the finding related to relevance serves as a manipulation check indicating that this manipulation did in fact impact perceptions of
relevance as planned such that those in the relevant condition felt the feedback was more relevant than those in the non-relevant condition.

Second, the non-relevant condition appeared to create feelings of confusion and frustration for participants, more so than the relevant condition.
Specifically, individuals receiving feedback that was not relevant felt less
competent and felt that the information was less accurate as well as less comprehensible. This begins to look at user's perceptions of the feedback loop
itself. Many feedback loops are obscured to users or perhaps even invisible.
When feedback loops create feelings of irrelevance, users start to become
aware of the feedback loop and its shortcomings.

Third, enjoyment was impacted by relevance such that relevance predicted
a more enjoyable experience. This highlights the importance of relevance in
the equation of media feedback. Indeed, relevance is vital to the function of
a feedback loop. Beyond that, the PROCESS macro showed that relevance
functioned through feelings of competence and perceptions of information
comprehensibility. In this case, key to getting people to enjoy media feedback
is to make it relevant as this, in turn, will make people feel better about their
ability and about the quality of the information they are receiving from the
system.

From here, the prescribed hierarchical regression was used. In step 1, age,
gender, race, income, photography expertise were entered. In step 2, feelings of discouragement, encouragement, competence, autonomy, relatedness,
information accuracy, cognitive load, surveillance, information comprehensibility, information comprehensiveness, and information relevance were
entered. In step 3, the condition was entered. Enjoyment was entered as the
dependent variable. These results are detailed in Table 8.1. This was run
twice more with meaningfulness entered as the dependent variable and entertainment entered as the dependent variable (Table 8.2 and 8.3).

Enjoyment was predicted by feelings of discouragement, encouragement,
competence, and autonomy. Enjoyment, then, was predicted entirely by the
way the individual felt. In other words, the media feedback was enjoyable
if it made the individual feel like he or she was capable, independent, and
supported.

Feelings of meaningfulness were predicted by encouragement, relatedness, and information accuracy. In this case, relationships with others were
critical to feelings of meaningfulness. Information quality was also a factor.
Participants found it important to ascribe meaning to the information presented and that was only possible if the information was comprehensive.

Table 8.1 Regression Analysis for Enjoyment

	B	SE	β
Step 1			
Gender	.12	.24	,04
Age	.00	.01	-.01
Race	-.03	.06	-.04
Income	.05	.03	.01
Photo Expert	.08	.07	.01
	$F(5, 184) = .88$		
	Adj. R2 = .00		
Step 2			
Gender	.07	.16	.02
Age	.00	,01	.03
Race	.01	.04	.01
Income	.01	.02	.03
Photo Expert	-.06	.05	-.07
Discouraging	-.11	.05	-.14[a]
Encouraging	.13	.05	.17[b]
Competence	.29	.08	.27[c]
Autonomy	.23	.08	.20[b]
Relatedness	.06	.06	.06
Cognitive Load	.03	.08	.03
Surveillance	.00	.06	.00
Information Accuracy	.12	.07	.14
Information Comprehensibility	.11	.09	.09
Information Comprehensiveness	.00	.07	-.01
Relevance	.08	.08	.09
	$F(11, 184) = 18.42$[c]		
	Adj. R2 = .60		
Step 3			
Gender	.07	.16	.02
Age	.00	.01	.03
Race	.01	.04	.01
Income	.01	.02	.03
Photo Expert	-.06	.05	-.07
Discouraging	-.11	.05	-.14[b]
Encouraging	.13	.05	.17[b]
Competence	.29	.08	.27[c]
Autonomy	.23	.08	.20[b]
Relatedness	.06	.06	.06
Cognitive Load	-.03	.08	-.03
Surveillance	.00	.06	.00
Information Accuracy	.12	.08	.14
Information Comprehensibility	.11	.09	.09
Information Comprehensiveness	.01	.07	.01
Relevance	.08	.08	.09
Condition	.01	.16	.05
	$F(1, 184) = 17.24$[c]		
	Adj. R2 = .60		

[a]$p < 0.05$. [b]$p < 0.01$, [c]$p < 0.001$. No superscript $p > 0.05$.

Table 8.2   Regression Analysis for Meaningfulness

	B	SE	β
Step 1			
Gender	.12	.24	,04
Age	.00	.01	-.01
Race	-.03	.06	-.04
Income	.05	.03	.01
Photo Expert	.08	.07	.01
	$F(5, 184) = .88$		
	Adj. $R^2 = .00$		
Step 2			
Gender	.07	.16	.02
Age	.00	.01	.03
Race	.01	.04	.01
Income	.01	.02	.03
Photo Expert	-.06	.05	-.07
Discouraging	-.11	.05	-.14[a]
Encouraging	.13	.05	.17[b]
Competence	.29	.08	.27[c]
Autonomy	.23	.08	.20[b]
Relatedness	.06	.06	.06
Cognitive Load	.03	.08	.03
Surveillance	.00	.06	.00
Information Accuracy	.12	.07	.14
Information Comprehensibility	.11	.09	.09
Information Comprehensiveness	.00	.07	-.01
Relevance	.08	.08	.09
	$F(11, 184) = 18.42^c$		
	Adj. $R^2 = .60$		
Step 3			
Gender	.07	.16	.02
Age	.00	.01	.03
Race	.01	.04	.01
Income	.01	.02	.03
Photo Expert	-.06	.05	-.07
Discouraging	-.11	.05	-.14[a]
Encouraging	.13	.05	.17[b]
Competence	.29	.08	.27[c]
Autonomy	.23	.08	.20[b]
Relatedness	.06	.06	.06
Cognitive Load	-.03	.08	-.03
Surveillance	.00	.06	.00
Information Accuracy	.12	.08	.14
Information Comprehensibility	.11	.09	.09
Information Comprehensiveness	.01	.07	.01
Relevance	.08	.08	.09
Condition	.01	.16	.05
	$F(1, 184) = 17.24^c$		
	Adj. $R^2 = .60$		

[a] $p < 0.05$. [b] $p < 0.01$, [c] $p < 0.001$. No superscript $p > 0.05$.

Table 8.3 Regression Analysis for Entertainment

	B	SE	β
Step 1			
Gender	-.11	.25	-.03
Age	.00	.01	.01
Race	.02	.07	.02
Income	.04	.03	.09
Photo Expert	.17	.07	.19[a]
	$F(5, 184) = 1.79$		
	Adj. $R^2 = .02$		
Step 2			
Gender	-.03	.19	-.01
Age	.00	.01	.00
Race	.06	.05	.07
Income	.00	.02	.01
Photo Expert	-.04	.06	-.05
Discouraging	-.18	.06	-.21[b]
Encouraging	.22	.06	.26[c]
Competence	.19	.09	.17[a]
Autonomy	.17	.09	.14
Relatedness	.17	.07	.17[a]
Cognitive Load	.12	.09	.10
Surveillance	-.04	.07	-.04
Information Accuracy	.11	.08	.11
Information Comprehensibility	-.13	.10	.11
Information Comprehensiveness	.27	.09	.28[b]
Relevance	-.09	.09	-.09
	$F(11, 184) = 13.42^c$		
	Adj. $R^2 = .52$		
Step 3			
Gender	-.02	.19	-.01
Age	.00	.01	.00
Race	.06	.05	.07
Income	.01	.03	.01
Photo Expert	-.04	.06	-.05
Discouraging	.10	.06	-.20[b]
Encouraging	.21	.05	.25[c]
Competence	.21	.09	.18[a]
Autonomy	.17	.09	.14
Relatedness	.16	.07	.16[a]
Cognitive Load	.12	.09	.10
Surveillance	-.04	.07	-.05
Information Accuracy	.14	.09	.15
Information Comprehensibility	.13	.10	.11
Information Comprehensiveness	.26	.09	.27[b]
Relevance	-.09	.09	.08
Condition	.21	.18	.06
	$F(1, 184) = 12.72^c$		
	Adj. $R^2 = .52$		

[a] $p < 0.05$. [b] $p < 0.01$, [c] $p < 0.001$. No superscript $p > 0.05$.

Feelings of entertainment were predicted by discouragement, encouragement, competence and autonomy, relatedness, and information comprehensiveness. Entertainment was predicted by a mixture of the items that predicted
enjoyment and meaningfulness. This provides evidence that entertainment
can be multifaceted such that it can be both enjoyable and meaningful (Oliver
et al., 2016).

This study shows the critical importance of relevance for media feedback.
This chapter examined relevance generated by media feedback. Exploring
how media feedback might leverage relevance inherent to the user is worth
exploring. Regardless, this chapter "pulled back the curtain" on feedback
systems for users. A user becomes aware of the feedback mechanism when
the mechanism produces non-relevant feedback. This can be perceived as
a malfunction by the user. This awareness is undesirable for users and thus
feedback loops should be designed carefully in order to engender relevance.
In that vein, this chapter also suggests that user perceptions of how feedback
systems work merits further study. The next chapter will look at another
example of how users perceive feedback systems to function and how that
influences their attitudes toward that media feedback.

Chapter 9

Media Feedback as Authority

The previous chapter suggested that when a feedback loop created feelings of irrelevance for the user, the user enjoyed the feedback less and it led to other negative psychological outcomes. The supposition was that when a feedback loop was not working properly (i.e., generated feelings of irrelevance), the user started to think about the nature of feedback and the way in which feedback is supposed to work—even if only at a subconscious or superficial level. This raises the question, why would users assume that feedback loops create feelings of relevance from them? This is a large assumption, and it is an assumption the current chapter aims to explore.

As discussed, endemic to a feedback loop is a goal. That is, a necessary condition for a feedback loop to exist is a desired outcome; otherwise, the feedback would not direct a user toward or away from certain behaviors. This is a distinct trait that separates feedback from other forms of media communication.

Simultaneously, media feedback fundamentally describes a dialogue between the user and the media interface. In media environments, user input is assessed by the interface and the interface, in turn, conveys information back to the user, communicating progress (or lack of progress) toward the desired goal. Then, the user's next input should incorporate this newly acquired information and the cycle repeats. In essence, the experience of using certain types of media effectively relies on feedback. Generally accepted is the assumption that feedback is used to enhance user performance or guide user behavior. This point is important because it conveys that the feedback loop "knows" something that the user does not necessarily know; otherwise, the feedback system would be redundant.

In other words, media are imbued with a sense of *authority* when providing feedback to users. Well-designed interfaces should make users trust that the feedback they are receiving will help them achieve goals. When feedback is irrelevant this authority is undermined, and the feedback loses efficacy. As a result, this chapter will examine how users perceive authority in media feedback.

As mentioned, much of the research on feedback has been done in educational settings. This is particularly salient when discussing authority because the typical classroom setting has inherent authority figures such that the instructor is tasked with correcting student behavior and improving student performance on clearly stated goals. The instructor has authority over the students and the course material. This is an often-overlooked aspect of feedback and one that should be carefully considered moving forward.

In a study examining second language writing courses, students were asked to rate the usefulness and preference for peer feedback or instructor feedback (Hu, 2019). Overall, feedback was noted to be useful in the classroom setting and, importantly, there was a strong preference for instructor feedback over peer feedback. This study did not directly test the notion of authority but the relevant inference from this is that students preferred feedback from an authority figure. This not only shows a preference for authority in feedback but perhaps also an expectation of authority embedded within feedback. Indeed, students often go to instructors for clarification, advice, guidance, etc. because students expect instructors to have the ability to answer questions with an authoritative knowledge base.

According to Riggio, Chaleff, and Lippman-Blumen (2008) leadership and followership are determined by authority such that a person in authority has the right to tell others what to do and the responsibility of an event ultimately is placed upon the authority figure. Riggio and colleagues also indicated that authority was related to several other concepts: assertiveness, aggressiveness, social and political skills, power, control, and leverage to name a few. Most of these concepts can be mapped onto media feedback in a multitude of ways.

For example, media feedback can assert itself into one's use of a platform. Assertion might be akin to frequency of feedback, and how it does so might be considered aggressive if it interrupts the user experience or if it uses harsh words, sounds, or visuals. Consider if a media platform showed the user a picture of suffering animals each time the user did not perform the requested task. That sort of aggressive feedback might be effective in guiding behavior but may not engender positive attitudes toward the platform. If feedback is implemented appropriately, feedback should also convey that it has the power to give the user certain affordances or allow the user to more effectively employ the platform. In that same capacity, feedback can leverage certain positions by using rewards for users in order to entice specific actions. Likewise, effective feedback is designed to control behavior such that it guides users. One might even argue that high-quality feedback demonstrates social and political skills through the way it interfaces with the user. For example, feedback might be considered socially or politically adept if it "understands" users and therefore positions itself favorably with the user. As a result, this book argues that critical leadership and followership concepts (Riggio, et al., 2008) can quite readily be mapped onto feedback.

Another area that is worth exploring with regard to feedback authority is the Elaboration Likelihood Model (ELM) (Petty & Cacioppo, 1979; Petty & Cacioppo, 1990; Petty, Cacioppo, & Schumann, 1983). The ELM is a theory of persuasion that argues there are two processes of persuasion, the central route and the peripheral route. If someone is invested in a particular topic, then he or she will take the central route and think about or elaborate upon messages that are presented to them. A result of this elaboration is the deepened impact of strong arguments. Conversely, if someone is not invested in a particular topic, they are more likely to take the peripheral route, paying less attention to the strength of arguments but instead rely on cues for opinions and attitudes. In other words, if people are not invested in a particular topic, they will be more impacted by cues because they are less willing to think about the arguments.

In many of the studies on the ELM, the source of the message has been used as a cue. For example, if a study used stimulus material related to a new health product, the study could use an authoritative source such as a doctor or a non-authoritative source such as a layperson. The doctor and the layperson could make the same argument and if someone is on the peripheral route then he or she would be more likely to be persuaded by the authoritative source than the non-authoritative source because he or she is relying on the cue as opposed to the argument.

This provides evidence that if feedback is authoritative, it should be effective in persuading audiences if they are not particularly invested in the topic or in lieu of argumentation. Consider an email digest that redirects users to political opinion articles on different websites. If the recipient of the email is invested in politics, he or she will likely make an assessment of the articles' main arguments to determine what and where they click. However, many people surf the internet or check their email casually and may not be particularly invested in what they are seeing. In this case, if the email came from a political expert as opposed to someone who is not an authority on politics, a user would be more likely to be persuaded to click to the linked site. The purpose of the current chapter is to apply this well-established area of research to feedback and the authority inherent therein.

METHOD

This chapter employed a 2-condition quasi-experiment testing the differences two different manifestations of authority in media feedback. In one condition, participants were asked to think about the system-generated feedback they receive when using a search engine such as Google. In the second condition, participants were asked to think about the system-generated feedback they receive when using a streaming service such as Amazon Prime or Netflix. While these methods of feedback are materially similar, there may be perceived differences in how they confer authority to the user based on content and presentation.

Specifically, participants read, "When I use search engines such as Google and I see the results, I feel that the results . . ." or "When I use a streaming service like Netflix or Amazon Prime, and I see that the platform has suggested things to watch based on my previous watching behavior I feel the suggestions . . ." From there, participants were asked to fill out a questionnaire detailing their attitudes and perceptions specific to their condition

MEASURES

This study included a few new additional measures related to authority. Specifically, Hinkin and Schriesheim's (1989) measures of power were adapted for use in this study. These included five types of power: reward power, coercive power, legitimate power, expert power, and referent power, each of which had multiple items. Reward power included "increase the value of the service," "influence my use of the service," "provide me with quality content," and "influence my personal development." Coercive power included "give me undesirable results/suggestions," "make my task difficult for me," "make things unpleasant," and "make the task distasteful." Legitimate Power included "make me feel that I have commitments to meet," "make me feel like I should look through the results/suggestions," "give me the feeling I have responsibilities to fulfill," and "make me recognize that I have tasks to accomplish." Expert power included "give me good suggestions," "share with me considerable expertise," "provide me with sound guidance," and "provide me with needed knowledge." Referent power included "make me feel valued," "make me feel approved of," "make me feel personally accepted," and "make me feel important."

A measure of leadership was adapted from Cronshaw and Lord (1987). This included, "lead me appropriately," "felt like a good leader for me," "I would use these results/suggestions to lead my decisions," and "to what extent are the results/suggestions representative of leader behavior such that you feel led by the results/suggestions."

Each of the measures indicated acceptable reliability (competence $\alpha = .91$, autonomy $\alpha = .86$, relatedness $\alpha = .93$, = surveillance $\alpha = .84$, information comprehensibility $\alpha = .85$, information comprehensiveness $\alpha = .87$, cognitive load $\alpha = .86$, leadership $\alpha = .91$, reward power $\alpha = .85$, coercive power $\alpha = .92$, legitimate power $\alpha = .86$, expert power $\alpha = .90$, referent power $\alpha = .96$). For information accuracy, the item, "The information in the tool is not precise" was removed and the remaining two items were correlated, $r = .66$, $p < .01$. Likewise, for relevance, the item, "The information in the tool does not help me at all" was removed and the remaining two items were correlated, $r = .69$, $p < .01$.

PARTICIPANTS

After removing participants who failed the attention checks, 197 remained. The participants were majority white (71.6%) females (50.8%) in their mid-30s ($M = 35.60$), and 53.3 percent made \$59,999 a year or less. The sample also used a search engine on average 11.22 times a day and 5.88 days a week on average using a streaming service.

RESULTS

Feelings of enjoyment, meaningfulness, entertainment, discouragement, encouragement, competence, autonomy, relatedness, information accuracy, cognitive load, surveillance, information comprehensibility, information comprehensiveness, information relevance, general leadership, reward power, coercive power, legitimate power, expert power, and referent power were entered as dependent variables. The condition, search engine results or streaming service results, was used as the independent variable. Age, gender, race, income, how often participants use search engines and streaming services were entered as covariates. This analysis revealed a multivariate effect of the search engine versus streaming service ($F(20, 166) = 3.37$, $p < .001$, Wilks' $\Lambda = .71$, $\eta_p^2 = .29$).

The individual ANOVAs related to platform significantly in impacted feelings of competence ($F(1, 185) = 4.13$, $p < .05$, $\eta_p^2 = .02$), search engine ($M = 5.43$, $SD = 1.25$, streaming $M = 5.03$, $SD = 1.22$), surveillance ($F(1, 185) = 14.84$, $p < .001$, $\eta_p^2 = .07$), search engine ($M = 5.69$, $SD = 1.16$), streaming ($M = 4.98$, $SD = 1.28$), leadership ($F(1, 185) = 9.39$, $p < .01$, $\eta_p^2 = .05$), search engine ($M = 5.36$, $SD = 1.09$), streaming ($M = 4.81$, $SD = 1.18$), reward power ($F(1, 185) = 12.44$, $p < .001$, $\eta_p2 = .06$), search engine ($M = 5.46$, $SD = 1.08$), streaming ($M = 4.8$, $SD = 1.20$), and expert power ($F(1, 185) = 15.02$, $p < .001$, $\eta_p2 = .07$), search engine ($M = 5.47$, $SD = 1.06$), and streaming ($M = 4.76$, $SD = 1.31$).

In each case, a search engine was viewed to have more authority and provide a greater degree of competence and surveillance to participants. Most importantly, this provides evidence that media feedback is viewed with authority as it can lead and has power over the user. Notably, there were also differences between search engines and streaming platforms indicating that how media feedback confers authority can differ significantly. This is likely due to the content and presentation. Suggestions from a streaming service likely feel less precise than search results from something the user has entered.

Given that the condition had no impact on any of the main outcomes (enjoyment, meaningfulness, and entertainment), the PROCESS macro was forgone and the prescribed hierarchical regression was used.

In step 1, age, gender, race, income, how often participants used search engines and streaming services were entered. In step 2, feelings of discouragement, encouragement, competence, autonomy, relatedness, information accuracy, cognitive load, surveillance, information comprehensibility, information comprehensiveness, information relevance, general leadership, reward power, coercive power, legitimate power, expert power, and referent power were entered. In step 3, the condition was entered. Enjoyment was entered as the dependent variable. These results are detailed in table 9.1. This was run twice more with meaningfulness entered as the dependent variable and entertainment entered as the dependent variable (table 9.2 and 9.3).

For the regression tables, the notion of authority was critical for feelings of enjoyment and meaningfulness but not entertainment. This again shows the importance of understanding media feedback as a system with authority, especially when examining desired outcomes or goals. Feelings of encouragement were also critical to media feedback. Overall, there is evidence that media feedback has the traits and qualities of an authority figure.

Table 9.1 Regression Analysis for Enjoyment

	B	SE	β
Step 1			
Gender	.15	.20	.05
Age	.00	.01	.01
Race	.15	.06	.17[a]
Income	.07	.03	.17[a]
Time spent with search engine	-.01	.01	-.06
Time spent streaming	.03	.02	.12
	$F(6, 186) = 2.22$[a]		
	Adj. $R^2 = .04$		
Step 2			
Gender	.13	.13	.04
Age	.01	.01	.06
Race	.06	.04	.07
Income	.02	.02	.04
Time spent with search engine	.01	.01	.05
Time spent streaming	-.01	.01	-.02
Discouraging	-.03	.05	-.05
Encouraging	.16	.05	.18[b]
Competence	.02	.08	.02
Autonomy	.12	.09	.10
Relatedness	-.00	.07	-.01
Cognitive Load	.17	.08	.16[a]
Surveillance	.26	.09	.23[b]
Information Accuracy	.14	.11	.11
Information Comprehensibility	.03	.11	.02
Information Comprehensiveness	.02	.14	.01
Relevance	.03	.11	.03
Leadership	.27	.11	.22[a]
Reward Power	.30	.12	.24[a]
Coercive Power	-.07	.06	-.08
Legitimate Power	-.11	.07	-.11
Expert Power	-.23	.11	-.20[b]
Referent Power	.07	.08	.08
	$F(17, 169)\ 11.75$[c]		
	Adj. $R^2 = .62$		
Step 3			
Gender	.11	.13	.04
Age	.01	.01	.06
Race	.07	.04	.08
Income	.01	.02	.03
Time spent with search engine	.01	.00	.04
Time spent streaming	-.00	.01	-.01
Discouraging	-.03	.05	-.05
Encouraging	.14	.05	.16[b]
Competence	.04	.08	.03
Autonomy	.10	.09	.08

(Continued)

Chapter 9

Table 9.1   Regression Analysis for Enjoyment (*Continued*)

	B	SE	β
Relatedness	-.02	.07	-.03
Cognitive Load	.18	.08	.17[a]
Surveillance	.29	.09	.25[c]
Information Accuracy	.11	.11	.09
Information Comprehensibility	.03	.11	.02
Information Comprehensiveness	.01	.14	.01
Relevance	.05	.11	.44
Leadership	.28	.11	.23[b]
Reward Power	.30	.12	.24[a]
Coercive Power	-.07	.06	-.08
Legitimate Power	-.11	.06	-.11
Expert Power	-.19	.11	-.17
Referent Power	.06	.08	.07
Condition	.27	.15	.09
	$F(1, 168) = 14.46^c$		
	Adj. $R^2 = .01$		

[a]$p < 0.05.$ [b]$p < 0.01,$ [c]$p < 0.001.$ No superscript $p > 0.05.$

Table 9.2 Regression Analysis for Meaningfulness

	B	SE	β
Step 1			
Gender	-.29	.23	-.09
Age	-.01	.01	-.07
Race	.08	.07	.07
Income	.02	.03	.05
Time spent with search engine	-.02	.01	-.16[a]
Time spent streaming	.06	.02	.25[c]
		$F(6, 186) = 3.00$[b]	
		Adj. $R^2 = .06$	
Step 2			
Gender	-.14	.16	-.04
Age	.00	.01	-.03
Race	-.01	.05	-.01
Income	-.03	.02	-.06
Time spent with search engine	.00	.01	.00
Time spent streaming	.02	.01	.06
Discouraging	.04	.06	.05
Encouraging	.21	.06	.21[b]
Competence	.08	.10	.06
Autonomy	.27	.11	.20[a]
Relatedness	-.11	.09	-.11
Cognitive Load	.05	.09	.05
Surveillance	-.02	.10	-.02
Information Accuracy	.10	.12	.07
Information Comprehensibility	-.10	.13	-.06
Information Comprehensiveness	.10	.13	.06
Relevance	-.15	.14	-.11
Leadership	.33	.13	.23[a]
Reward Power	-.27	.15	-.19
Coercive Power	-.13	.08	-.14
Legitimate Power	.14	.08	.13
Expert Power	.29	.13	.22[a]
Referent Power	.23	.10	.24[a]
		$F(17, 100)$ 10.04[c]	
		Adj. $R^2 = .60$	
Step 3			
Gender	-.14	.16	-.04
Age	.00	.01	-.03
Race	-.01	.05	-.01
Income	-.03	.02	-.06
Time spent with search engine	.00	.01	.00
Time spent streaming	.02	.01	.06
Discouraging	.04	.06	.05
Encouraging	.20	.06	.20[b]
Competence	.08	.10	.06
Autonomy	.27	.11	.20[a]

(Continued)

Table 9.2   Regression Analysis for Meaningfulness (*Continued*)

	B	SE	β
Relatedness	-.11	.09	-.12
Cognitive Load	.06	.10	.05
Surveillance	-.02	.10	-.01
Information Accuracy	.09	.13	.06
Information Comprehensibility	-.10	.13	-.06
Information Comprehensiveness	.10	.17	.06
Relevance	-.15	.14	-.11
Leadership	.33	.13	.26[a]
Reward Power	.-26	.15	-.18
Coercive Power	-.13	.08	-.13
Legitimate Power	.14	.08	.13
Expert Power	.30	.13	.23[a]
Referent Power	.23	.10	.24[a]
Condition	-.06	.17	-.02
	$F(1, 168) = 12.72^c$		
	Adj. $R^2 = .60$		

[a]$p < 0.05$. [b]$p < 0.01$, [c]$p < 0.001$. No superscript $p > 0.05$.

Table 9.3 Regression Analysis for Entertainment

	B	SE	β
Step 1			
Gender	-.11	.21	-.04
Age	-.01	.01	-.08
Race	.05	.06	.06
Income	.06	.03	.13
Time spent with search engine	-.02	.01	-.17[a]
Time spent streaming	.04	.02	.18[a]
	$F(6, 186) = 2.49$[a]		
	Adj. $R^2 = .04$		
Step 2			
Gender	-.10	.15	-.04
Age	.00	.01	-.03
Race	-.01	.05	-.01
Income	.01	.02	.03
Time spent with search engine	.00	.01	-.04
Time spent streaming	.00	.01	.02
Discouraging	.06	.06	.08
Encouraging	.26	.06	.28[c]
Competence	.02	.09	.02
Autonomy	.24	.11	.19[a]
Relatedness	.17	.08	.19[a]
Cognitive Load	.07	.09	.07
Surveillance	.04	.01	.03
Information Accuracy	.06	.12	.05
Information Comprehensibility	.05	.13	.03
Information Comprehensiveness	-.11	.16	-.08
Relevance	.04	.13	.03
Leadership	.26	.12	.20[a]
Reward Power	.10	.14	.08
Coercive Power	-.13	.07	-.15
Legitimate Power	-.04	.07	-.04
Expert Power	-.06	.12	-.04
Referent Power	-.02	.09	-.02
	$F(17, 169) = 11.15$[c]		
	Adj. $R^2 = .56$		
Step 3			
Gender	-.13	.15	-.04
Age	.00	.01	-.03
Race	-.01	.05	-.01
Income	.01	.02	.02
Time spent with search engine	-.01	.01	-.05
Time spent streaming	.01	.01	.04
Discouraging	.06	.06	.08
Encouraging	.23	.06	.25[c]
Competence	.08	.10	.06
Autonomy	.05	.09	.04

(Continued)

Table 9.3   Regression Analysis for Entertainment (*Continued*)

	B	SE	β
Relatedness	.13	.08	.15
Cognitive Load	.08	.09	.08
Surveillance	.08	.10	.07
Information Accuracy	.02	.12	.01
Information Comprehensibility	.05	.12	.04
Information Comprehensiveness	-.12	.15	-.09
Relevance	.06	.13	.05
Leadership	.29	.12	.23[a]
Reward Power	.11	.14	.08
Coercive Power	-.13	.07	-.15
Legitimate Power	-.03	.07	-.03
Expert Power	.01	.12	.01
Referent Power	-.04	.09	-.04
Condition	-.45	.16	-.15[b]
	$F_{(1, 168)} = 11.73$[c]		
	Adj. $R^2 = .57$		

[a]$p < 0.05$. [b]$p < 0.01$, [c]$p < 0.001$. No superscript $p > 0.05$.

Chapter 10

Distractions and Media Feedback

The previous chapter argued that media feedback is effective when it is perceived as an authority and, under the ELM, users are likely to perceive an authority cue from media feedback. As discussed, cues become more effective the less a person thinks about a message. Consequently, the cues that a user receives from messages will be more pronounced when the user is distracted and unable to think too much about the content. This chapter will explore the role of distractions on the efficacy of media feedback.

While examining media feedback distraction appears to be particularly important alongside progress information. These are both germane to media feedback because the effects of feedback are intertwined with distractions, and progress information with regard to attitude toward content and performance on a task (Drolet & Luce, 2004; Fishbach & Dhar, 2005; Huang & Zhang, 2011; Ward & Mann, 2000). Specifically, progress information should increase positive attitudes and improve performance while distraction should do the inverse.

One reason that studying distraction alongside media feedback is the media landscape itself. In media environments, people commonly switch between media formats on an average of four times per minute (Brasel & Gips, 2011). Thus, when people are in media feedback loops, they are likely distracted from them. This "cognitive overload"—the prevailing state when the user's capacity for mental processes is depleted—is one of the main challenges of creating effective media feedback (Mayer & Moreno, 2003). Cognitive capacity is often depleted when two or more cognitive processes are in opposition and cognitive resources become scarce resulting in user distraction (Sweller, 1988). This is the norm rather than the exception for many media consumers.

Distractions, like a chiming smartphone or a new email, are commonly encountered while using media (Brasel & Gips, 2011) and should negatively impact the efficacy of task performance (Drolet & Luce, 2004; Lamble, Kauranen, Laakso, & Summala, 1999; Ward & Mann, 2000). These deleterious effects likely extend to feedback. Indeed, the effects of distractions on media feedback efficacy are similar to those of ineffective feedback broadly (Carver & Scheier, 2001; Diclemente et al., 2001; Hattie & Timperlay, 2007; Kluger & DeNisi, 1996).

To accurately explore the effects of distractions on media feedback, researchers can create conditions of distractions in a lab setting in order to induce cognitive load with secondary tasks such as digit memorization (Drolet & Luce, 2004; Shiv & Huber, 2000; Ward & Mann, 2000). These memorization tasks adequately distract individuals and detract from goals (Drolet & Luce, 2004; Lamble, Kauranen, Laakso, & Summala, 1999; Ward & Mann, 2000).

Given the important role of progress information in media feedback (Connellan & Zemke, 1993, Fleming & Levie, 1993; Kluger & DeNisi, 1996), examining distraction in concert with progress information may help uncover significant effects of media feedback. Thus, this chapter examines the interplay of distraction and progress information.

Progress is movement toward a defined goal (Fishbach & Dhar, 2005; Hawkins, Lambert, Vermeersch, Slade, & Tuttle, 2004). Progress information, then, is a representation or communication of movement toward a goal. In the domain of media feedback, progress information has been tied to notions of usability (Crystal & Kalyanaraman, 2004; Nielsen, 1998). Usability is broadly defined as the ease with which a system can be used (Nielsen, 2003). As such, progress information helps show users how to improve performance and, thus, makes the system simpler to use. With regard to media feedback, progress information, when facing the user, communicates the discrepancy between goal and performance (Ashby, 1956; Goetz, 2011; Carver & Scheier, 2001).

In empirical studies, progress information has been varied by presentation speed (Card, Robertson, & Mackinlay, 1991) and method of presentation (Hawkins et al., 2004). Progress information displays have also been varied by percent-done indication (Myers, 1985), a progress bar, or ambiguous signs of advancement like a spinning ball or moving disc (Nielsen, 1998). In video games, progress information is given to players when they succeed or fail in order to help them confirm their actions or correct their missteps (Gee, 2005; Juul, 2010). Role-playing games award players with experience points that allow them to "level up" their characters. This is often presented as a fraction (10,000/40,000 experience points) like in *World of Warcraft*. In other cases, progress is denoted with meters that fill when specific actions meet goals like in *Gears of War 5* and *Overwatch*. Games also keep score to show how well a player has performed against other players and against past performances.

In feedback literature, progress information has been deemed critical for increasing positive attitudes and improving performance (Connellan & Zemke, 1993, Fleming & Levie, 1993; Gee, 2005; Hawkins et al., 2004; Kluger & DeNisi, 1996; Ramsay, Barbesi, & Preece, 1998; Schunk & Swartz, 1993). Most notably, progress information varies in terms of level of advancement communicated such that different levels of progress should impact performance on tasks and attitudes toward content differentially. Particularly, progress information that indicates little movement toward a goal can make users feel that a task is difficult and therefore engenders negative attitudes and impedes task performance (Huang & Zhang, 2011). On the other hand, progress information that suggests imminent goal completion encourages the perception that the task can be easily and effortlessly accomplished (Fishbach & Dhar, 2005).

When considering the nuances, the effects of progress information have largely been explained through motivation and self-esteem. The motivation to pursue goals increases and decreases based on the progress information presented (Zhang & Huang, 2010). Not surprisingly, high motivation is tied to improved performance on goals and more favorable attitudes toward content while low motivation is linked to worse performance and less favorable attitudes.

Progress information also impacts performance and attitudes through self-esteem (Hattie & Timperley, 2007; Schunk & Pajares, 2002). If people are told they have done well (made considerable progress), they will feel better about themselves. The inverse is also accurate. Accordingly, those experiencing low (high) self-esteem will harbor negative (positive) attitudes toward content and have less (more) improved performance (Hattie & Timperley, 2007; Schunk, 1991; 1995). Moreover, those experiencing high self-esteem demonstrate more persistence on tasks, which should further improve task performance (Baumeister, 1998; Schunk, 1995).

Media feedback that includes progress information is not likely a panacea for distractions (Brasel & Gips, 2011) but the negative effects of distraction could be blunted when feedback indicates high progress because it is more motivating and increases self-esteem. However, if progress information indicates low progress and lowers motivation and self-esteem, the effects of distraction might be strengthened.

METHOD

Please note that this chapter does not use the method and measures outlined previously in this book. The design of the study for this chapter implemented a 2 (distraction: low and high) x 4 (progress information: no

progress information, low progress, medium progress, high progress) factorial experiment. This study was performed in a lab setting due to the intrica-
cies of the procedure. Participants played a researcher-designed game called
Spare Change! In this game, dollar bills and bombs fell from the top of the
screen. The object of the game was to move the dollar signs into a "bank"
bin and the bombs into a "trash" bin on the bottom of the screen. Participants
read the following description of the game: "You must guide falling dollar
signs into the bank bin at the bottom of the screen. Different dollar signs
are worth different values. Also, make sure you throw bombs into the trash
or they will decrease the money you have collected!" The dollar values that
fell from the top of the screen were: $1, $5, $10, $20 and $50. The size of
the dollar bill corresponded to the dollar amount ($1 was smallest, $50 was
largest).

Participants in the high distraction condition were asked to memorize an
eight-digit number while participants in the low distraction condition memorized a two-digit number (Drolet & Luce, 2004; Shiv & Huber, 2000; Ward &
Mann, 2000). Numbers were generated using an online random number generator. After playing the game participants were asked to recall the number
they were asked to memorize. If participants could not accurately recall the
digit string, then they were eliminated from analysis as this reflected a lack
of dedicating cognitive resources to memorization and, ultimately, a lack of
manipulation efficacy.

In the "no progress information" condition participants received no information on their progress toward the game goal. In the low, medium, and high
progress conditions participants were told they had completed 20 percent,
50 percent or 80 percent of the game goal, respectively. These values were
pretested prior to the experiment with twenty-five participants.

Three items based on Fishbach and Dhar (2005) and Huang and Zhang
(2011) were used to evaluate *perceived progress*. Items were measured on
a 9-point Likert-type scale where 1 represented "strongly disagree" and 9
represented "strongly agree." Sample items included, "I have made a lot
of progress toward the game goal." This scale demonstrated high reliability ($\alpha = .92$) and there were significant differences between groups, ($F(2,
23) = 55.42, p < .001, \eta^2 = .85$). According to a post hoc analysis using a
Bonferroni correction, those receiving high progress information ($M = 8.00,
SD = 1.00$) perceived more progress toward their goal than those receiv-
ing low progress information ($M = 2.37, SD = .92 , p < .001$) and medium
progress information ($M = 4.75, SD = 1.16, p < .001$). Likewise, those in
the low progress condition perceived less progress than those in the medium
progress condition ($p < .01$).

For experimental control, progress information was displayed based on
assigned condition, not based on the players' actual performance. Actual

performance was obscured to the player but recorded to a remote server for analysis by the researcher. Regardless, participants were led to believe the manipulated progress information accurately reflected their performance. Player performance was further obscured to the participants by including more dropping dollar signs and bombs than the player could accurately keep track of (five per second), and by including descriptions of point calculations that made real time assessment difficult. In a pretest with ten participants, this manipulation proved satisfactory as none of the participants could accurately decipher their score.

During the experiment, participants played two levels of the game. Often, games are split into "levels" where different levels represent different challenges or sections of the game. This is a common practice for older games such as *Galaxian* and *Pac-Man* as well as newer games like *Doom Eternal* and *Candy Crush Saga*. Using two levels allowed players to enter a feedback loop and receive information from the game after level one but before level two.

Once participants completed level one and received feedback information, they filled out a pencil and paper questionnaire that assessed the dependent variables (with the exception of game performance which was assessed with a measure of actual performance change on level two). Upon leaving the facility, participants were fully debriefed regarding the nature of the experiment and the deception related to the game rewards.

MEASURES

Attitude toward the game was measured with an 11-item scale adapted from Kalyanaraman and Sundar (2006) ($\alpha = .95$). *Game performance* was assessed through player score on level two. Level one served as a baseline measure of performance before the player received any feedback information. Performance on level two was analyzed for improvement or decline from level one. *Game performance* was assessed with two variables: cash collected (approach behavior) and bombs collected (avoid behavior). The attitude scale demonstrated high reliability ($\alpha = .95$).

Perceived relevance was also measured with a six-item scale adapted from Kalyanaraman and Sundar (2006). *Motivation* was assessed with a six-item scale adapted from Harter (1981). *Attention* was measured with an 8-item scale adapted from Baer, Smith, and Allen (2004). Both perceived relevance and motivation displayed high reliability ($\alpha = .86$ and .90, respectively). The eight-item scale measuring attention demonstrated low reliability ($\alpha = .48$), consequently, a factor analysis was performed and revealed two items had low factor loadings. Those items were removed when summing the other six items. The remaining items exhibited moderate reliability (α = .78).

Self-esteem was measured using Rosenberg's (1965) 10-item scale. Items were measured on a 7-point Likert-type scale where 1 represented "strongly disagree" and 7 represented "strongly agree." Sample items included, "I feel that I have a number of good qualities" and "I feel I do not have much to be proud of (reverse coded)." The self-esteem scale demonstrated high reliability (α = .88).

A series of control measures were also included in the questionnaire beyond those listed in the previous chapters. Namely, *multitasking ability*, *game experience* and *perceived game skill* were assessed. These measures were included based on prior research on effects of play (Boot, Kramer, Simons, Fabiani, & Gratton, 2008; Green & Bavelier, 2003; Okagaki & Frensch, 1996; Prensky, 2001).

PARTICIPANTS

One hundred thirty-nine (N = 139) participants were recruited from a large mid-Atlantic public university. The majority of participants were women (82.00%), Caucasian (83.50%), and between the ages of nineteen and twenty-two years old (95.70%), M = 20.53, SD = 1.10. Participants were evenly distributed across conditions.

For a manipulation check, the *perceived progress* scale described in the pretest was used but for the main experiment items were measured on a 7-point Likert-type scale where 1 represented "strongly disagree" and 7 represented "strongly agree." This scale demonstrated high reliability (α = .89).

A one-way analysis of variance (ANOVA) revealed a statistically significant effect for the progress manipulation, $F(3, 130)$ = 4.06, $p < .01$, η^2 = .09. A follow-up post hoc analysis using a Bonferroni correction indicated that participants in the low progress condition (M = 2.78, SD = 1.46) perceived significantly less progress than those in the medium progress condition (M = 3.38, SD = 1.35, $p < .05$) and those in the high progress condition (M = 3.64, SD = 1.59, $p < .05$). Those in the medium progress condition had lower perceptions of progress than those in the high progress condition ($p < .05$). The no progress information was omitted from this particular analysis as there was no relevant data.

As for the distraction manipulation, nine participants were unable to accurately recall the digit string. These participants were eliminated from analysis and were not included among the stated 139 participants.

RESULTS

In order to assess the impact of distraction and progress information one ANCOVA and two ANOVAs were run. The ANCOVA was run with progress information and distraction entered as fully crossed independent factors. Gender, age, race, multitasking ability, game experience, and perceived game skill were included as covariates. Attitude toward the game was entered as the outcome. In both ANOVAs, progress information and distraction were entered as fully crossed independent factors. In one, cash collected was entered as the outcome variable and in the other, bombs collected was entered as the outcome variable. All covariates had no impact on the analyses.

There were no effects of distraction on attitude toward the game according to the ANCOVA ($F(1, 120) = .06, p = .81, \eta_p^2 = .00$, low distraction $M = 3.20$, $SD = 1.08$, high distraction $M = 3.06, SD = 1.19$). After running the ANOVAs on game performance, there was no significant difference for bombs collected ($F(3, 131) = .71, p =. 40, \eta_p^2 = .00$, low distraction $M = -1.44, SD = 7.73$, high distraction $M = -.46, SD = 6.55$). But there was a significant difference for cash collected ($F(1, 133) = 4.22, p = .04, \eta_p^2 = .03$). Importantly, the means were in the opposite direction of what was expected such that those experiencing low distraction played worse ($M = -6.12, SD = 14.55$) than those experiencing high distraction ($M = -1.66, SD = 13.24$).

With regard to progress information, the ANCOVA revealed that progress information did have a significant effect on attitude toward the game, ($F(3, 133) = 3.14, p < .05, \eta_p^2 = .07$). However, a follow-up post hoc analysis using a Bonferroni correction revealed a different pattern from what was expected. Participants in the "no progress information" condition ($M = 3.64, SD = 0.92$) had significantly more positive attitudes toward the video game than those in the low ($M = 2.98, SD = 1.16, p < .05$), medium ($M = 2.91, SD = 1.16, p < .05$) and high ($M = 3.01, SD = 1.15, p < .05$) progress conditions. The other conditions did not differ significantly.

The ANOVAs revealed there were no main effects on game performance for cash collected or bombs collected. There were also no significant interaction effects.

However, progress information had a significant effect on perceived relevance, ($F(3, 134) = 4.01, p < .05, \eta_p^2 = .08$), no progress ($M = 3.54, SD = 1.03$), low progress ($M = 3.43, SD = 1.30$), medium progress ($M = 2.66, SD = 1.00$), high progress ($M = 3.06, SD = 1.21$). The differences were mainly driven by the medium progress condition which significantly differed from the no progress and the low progress conditions.

Distraction yielded effects on attention, ($F(1, 136) = 2.29, p < .05, \eta_p^2 = .02$), and self-esteem, ($F(1, 137) = 3.64, p < .05, \eta_p^2 = .05$). Those in the low distraction condition paid more attention ($M = 4.85, SD = 1.14$) and had more self-esteem ($M = 6.00$, $SD = .90$) than those in the high distraction condition (attention $M = 4.51$, $SD = 1.06$, esteem $M = 5.76$, $SD = .86$).

The PROCESS macro (Hayes, 2012) was then used to test the role of potential mediating variables using model 8 with 2,000 bootstrap samples and 95 percent CI. The independent variables were progress information and distraction. The outcome variable was attitude. Gender, age, race, multitasking ability, game experience and perceived game skill were included as covariates. Attention, perceived relevance, and self-esteem were included as potential mediators. Motivation was removed from analysis as it demonstrated no significant results in previous analysis. Results indicated that progress information had a direct effect on attitude (point estimate $= -.16$, Boot SE $= .07$, $p < .05$) but there were no indirect effects for any of the mediators. There were no direct or indirect effects of distraction on attitude.

In order to test game performance outcomes, the previously described analysis using the PROCESS macro (Hayes, 2012) was used again with game performance entered as the outcome variable. This analysis was performed twice, once for cash collected and once for bombs collected. There were no direct effects of the independent variables but there was an indirect effect of distractions on cash collected via attention (point estimate $= .11$, Boot SE $= .08$, CI [.01, .35]).

The results showed that distraction had no impact on attitude toward the game. Overall, the game did not receive positive evaluations as participants ranked the game as low quality ($M = 2.15$, $SD = 1.08$). As a result, the addition of a distraction may not have been capable of lowering positive attitudes that were already quite low to begin with.

However, those experiencing low distraction had a steeper decline in performance from level one to level two than those experiencing high distraction. Of course, this finding was only observed for the "cash collected" measure and not for the "bombs collected" measure. One possible explanation is that high distraction may have distracted participants from most negative cognitions about the game. That is, high distractions may have prevented players from dwelling on aspects of the game they found unsatisfactory and, instead, encouraged them to focus on performing the primary game task. In other words, distraction made the game seem better.

Notably, participants' performance decreased in both conditions from level 1 to level 2 but there was less of a decrease for those experiencing high distraction. Thus, the expected effects of distraction on task performance may actually be inverted when the primary task is not viewed positively. This is noteworthy for distractions and media feedback when a task is viewed unfavorably.

The fact that this relationship was found for cash collected but not bombs collected also suggests that players were perhaps more likely to adhere to approach behaviors rather than avoid behaviors under conditions of high distraction. When players were highly distracted, they likely did not think much about the game and were more likely to follow the games instructions on "auto-pilot" (Csikszentmihalyi, 1990; Lewis & Linder, 1997). Approach behaviors, like collecting cash in this game, might qualify as a "thoughtless task" that benefits from distractions while other tasks that require more thought, like behaviors to prevent negative outcomes, do not garner the same benefit from distractions.

Analysis also revealed that those in the "no progress information" condition had more favorable attitudes toward the game than those in any of the other progress conditions. Interestingly, feedback literature suggests that clear progress information is superior to a lack of progress information (Connellan & Zemke, 1993, Fleming & Levie, 1993; Kluger & DeNisi, 1996). However, these findings show that "no progress" information might have advantages over clear progress information in media feedback. This finding is not completely original as it has been noted in other studies (Schunk, 1990; Soman & Shi, 2003) and it does indicate that progress information might elicit positive attitudes differently when it is presented in different contexts. In this case, it is possible that progress information made game play more task-oriented as opposed to entertainment-oriented, which diminished attitudes toward the game. Or it is possible that progress information, regardless of how much or how little progress was displayed, communicated failure to the participant while the "no progress" condition did not and thus every player was a "winner."

Progress information had no main effect on game performance. This further and perhaps more deeply challenges the claim that clear progress information is more effective than the lack of progress information (Connellan & Zemke, 1993, Fleming & Levie, 1993; Kluger & DeNisi, 1996). Again, this highlights the need to explore different types of progress information in different contexts within the realm of media feedback. These considerations could help to explain inconsistent effects of media feedback—context matters greatly.

The results also revealed no significant interaction effects. There was no interplay between progress information and distraction. This suggests that the impact of progress information and distraction on the outcome variables do not depend on one another. This was another unexpected finding as one might expect distraction to keep progress information from having an impact on users.

Lastly, this chapter explored how the effects of progress information and distraction on attitude toward the game and game performance were mediated by motivation, perceived relevance, attention, and self-esteem.

Analysis on potential mediators revealed that progress information only had a significant effect on perceived relevance, not on motivation, attention, or self-esteem. Perceived relevance was significantly lower for those in the medium progress condition than those in the no and low progress conditions. Thus, different levels of progress prompted different feelings of relevance. When progress was low, it conveyed to players that they needed to improve. Perhaps progress information indicating low progress was more relevant because it was perceived to more clearly provide guidance on how to play the game while higher progress information indicated that the player could simply continue on the same path without much guidance thus rendering the information irrelevant.

The same analysis on potential mediators revealed that distractions had a significant effect on self-esteem and attention. Specifically, those who were less distracted had higher self-esteem and paid more attention to the game. These findings are the most intuitive in the entire chapter. When someone is challenged with a difficult task, in this case a degree of distraction, the person is more likely to have lower self-esteem in the face of that challenge. Simultaneously, when someone is less distracted by another task, he or she is more likely to focus on the primary task, in this case playing the game.

As for the tests of mediation, progress information had a direct effect on attitude but there were no indirect effects through any of the mediators. This suggests that the impact of progress information on attitude was not explained by motivation, perceived relevance, attention or self-esteem, just progress information. However, as discussed, higher progress information lead to worse attitudes toward the game.

In terms of game performance, there were no direct effects of the independent variables on game performance, but there was an indirect effect of distraction on cash collected via attention. In other words, distraction impacted the amount of attention a player committed to the game. That level of attention impacted the performance in terms of cash collected. However, this effect showed that lower attention, not greater, enhanced performance. This shows that lack of attention might be beneficial in certain instances.

What readers should take away from this chapter is that progress information and distractions can impact how media feedback is received by users. However, readers should also be cognizant of the context of the findings with regard other studies on progress information and distractions. The context of progress information and distractions may be as important as progress information and distractions themselves when considering media feedback.

In conjunction with the previous chapter, this helps show that feedback might serve as a more effective cue when participants are distracted. Given the unexpected and, at times, vexing results of this chapter, a follow-up study was performed.

Chapter 11

Customization and Media Feedback

This relevance chapter examined feelings of relevance generated by media feedback. This chapter will explore customized feedback and, thereby, how media feedback might leverage an individual's inherent relevance. Likewise, this chapter is a natural follow up to the chapter on distractions. Since the distraction findings could be interpreted in a variety of ways both consistent and inconsistent with existing literature, this chapter aims to clarify some of that confusion through the lens of enhanced relevance.

One possible reason for the prevailing inconsistencies in feedback literature is that feedback is presented in a "one size fits all" style, thereby failing to consider users' unique attributes. Conceptually, this does not meet the standard of feedback as there must be some degree of relevance in the loop for it to be effective or for it to be considered feedback at all. True feedback loops address user performance for the individual not broad segmentation of the user population based on performance, however, the two are not mutually exclusive (see Noar, Benac, & Harris, 2007; Park, McDaniel, & Jung, 2009).

The supposition that addressing distinctive characteristics of the individual user is important has received tremendous support in various new media domains demonstrating that highly personalized content engenders more positive attitudes toward content (Briñol & Petty, 2006; Celsi & Olson, 1988; Kalyanaraman & Sundar, 2008; Kamali & Loker, 2002; Simonson, 2005; Valenzuela & Dhar, 2004) as well as greater adherence to intended behaviors (Adriaanse, de Ridder, & de Wit, 2009; Ansari & Mela, 2003; Emmons et al., 2004; Pelletier & Sharp, 2008; Rimer & Kreuter, 2006; Wan, 2008; Webb, Simmons, & Brandon, 2005).

Not surprisingly, modern media too offers substantial personalization like broad control over social media appearance, email signatures, profile pictures, and character customization in video games (see *Call of Duty, Rocket*

League) or level customization in video games (see *Super Mario Maker, Roblox*). Consequently, the current chapter tests the fundamental possibility that customized media feedback would be effective and perceived more favorably than generic or non-customized media feedback.

Given the earlier chapter on distraction and the robust evidence of the effects of customization, this chapter looks at customized media feedback alongside distraction. In this chapter, the effects of customized media feedback are analyzed under varying levels of distraction. The underlying argument is that relevance is critical to the efficacy of media feedback and customization is an effective method for generating relevance for users in a media feedback loop.

Customization can be described as creating messages for individual users (Kalyanaraman & Sundar, 2006). In contrast, generic messages are intended for all audience members without differentiation (Noar et al., 2007). Often, terms like personalization, matching, tailoring, and customization are used interchangeably in different disciplines (Hawkins et al., 2008; Latimer, Katulak, Mowad, & Salovey, 2005; Lustria, Cortese, Noar, & Glueckauf, 2009; Noar et al., 2007; Park et al., 2009; Rimer & Kreuter, 2006; Sundar & Marathe, 2010). While these terms do have nuanced definitions, their overarching meanings are largely the same: they all refer to individualized content (Kalyanaraman & Sundar, 2006; Wheeler, Petty, & Bizer, 2005; Wheeler, DeMarree, & Petty, 2008) that caters to "some aspect of the self" (Briñol & Petty, 2006, p. 583). In the current media environment, customization is common.

Generally, feedback is assumed to positively impact attitudes toward content and performance on goal-related tasks. Customization literature reveals similar outcomes (Ansari & Mela, 2003; Briñol & Petty, 2006; Carver & Scheier, 2001; Connellan & Zemke, 1993; Gee, 2005; Hattie & Timperley, 2007; Hawkins et al., 2008; Juul, 2010; Kalyanaraman & Sundar, 2006; Latimer et al., 2005; Malone, 1981; Ramaprasad, 1983; Reeves & Read, 2009). However, as noted, the empirical support for effects of feedback is far less consistent than the largely uniform empirical support for customization. Despite the widespread assumption that feedback increases positive attitudes and improves performance, nearly a third of feedback studies show no effects of feedback or the inverse of expected effects (Kluger & DeNisi, 1996).

Findings are typically less consistent when: users cannot isolate a relevant goal within feedback loops, users do not perceive feedback to be directly applicable (Carver & Scheier, 2001; Hattie & Timperley, 2007), and when feedback does not encourage user focus (Diclemente et al., 2001; Kluger & DeNisi, 1996). In light of these inconsistent findings, the unifying theme appears to be that feedback is ineffective when it does not address relevance to the individual or when the user is distracted. In each instance, customized media feedback could address the shortcomings, and potentially reconcile the inconsistencies, resulting in more positive attitudes and also improved performance. As for distractions, they *should* have deleterious effects on the efficacy of customized media feedbacks (Brasel & Gips, 2011; Hattie & Timperley, 2007; Kluger & DeNisi, 1996; Mayer & Moreno, 2003; Sweller, 1988).

Like the previous chapter and drawing from existing research on customization and feedback, the proposition is that customized feedback functions through increased attention, motivation, and relevance.

There is considerable support that customization can improve performance and increase positive attitudes via attention (Ansari & Mela, 2003; Hawkins et al. 2008; Rimer & Kreuter, 2006; Wheeler et al. 2005), motivation (Briñol & Petty, 2006; Celsi & Olson, 1988; Pelletier & Sharp, 2008; Rimer & Kreuter, 2006; Ruiter et al., 2006; Wheeler et al., 2008), and perceived relevance (Lavie, Sela, Oppenheim, Inbar, & Meyer, 2010; Petty & Cacioppo, 1990; Wheeler et al., 2008; Wheeler et al., 2005; Williams-Piehota et al., 2009). However, the support for feedback functioning through these mechanisms is mainly theoretical, not empirical (Bowman, 1982; Connellan & Zemke, 1993; Glanz et al., 2010; Gee, 2005; Hattie & Timperley, 2007; Hawkins et al., 2008; Kluger & DeNisi, 1996). Thus, more direct observations of these effects would develop an understanding of how customized media feedback functions.

By extending the principles of customization to media feedback, media feedback should benefit from the effects of customization. Specifically, customized media feedback should be more effective than non-customized feedback at improving performance and users should have more positive attitudes toward the content when the feedback is customized.

METHOD

Please note that this chapter does not use the method and measures outlined previously in this book. This study implemented a 2 (distraction: low and high) x 3 (feedback type: customized, non-customized, and no feedback) design.

Participants played the same researcher-designed game from the distraction chapter. In the customized feedback condition, players received feedback information in the form of a performance summary page. The feedback contained information based on individual preferences of each player. In the non-customized feedback condition, players received the same performance summary page with no individual differences acknowledged. In the no-feedback condition, players played the game with no indication of their performance via performance summary page. Regardless of condition, game play mechanics remained identical.

Importantly, feedback was manipulated to experimentally control for differences in performance. In this study, all participants—regardless of whether they were competent players or not—received an identically valenced performance evaluation.

Based on procedures suggested by Kalyanaraman and Sundar (2006), a pre-questionnaire was issued to participants two weeks ahead of their participation in the main experiment to allow for feedback information to be suitably customized to the individual. Once this data was collected, individual versions of the game were created for those randomly assigned to the customized feedback condition. The game was designed specifically for each participant such that when they entered their email address into the game, a unique version of the game was loaded for the player. The pre-questionnaire asked about participants' favorite foods, sports teams, musicians, etc. If in the customized condition, participants were told that they were eligible to win a gift card to whatever was listed as a favorite. For example, "Your score makes you eligible to win a gift card to see the New York Mets." In the non-customized condition, the message was generic, "Your score makes you eligible to win a gift card for tickets to a sporting event." Participants could not actually win the gift cards but were led to believe that they could.

A pretest with twenty-five participants demonstrated that participants perceived the customized feedback ($M = 7.44$, $SD = 1.77$) to be more "customized" than non-customized feedback ($M = 3.40$, $SD = 2.25$), $F(1, 22) = 23.31$, $p < .001$, $\eta^2 = .72$. Also, participants did not perceive the customized feedback prizes to be any more or less valuable in dollars than the non-customized feedback prizes.

The same distraction task from the distraction chapter was used in this chapter. Participants in the high distraction condition memorized an eight-digit number while participants in the low distraction condition memorized a two-digit number (Drolet & Luce, 2004; Shiv & Huber, 2000; Ward & Mann, 2000). Numbers were generated using an online random number generator.

During the main experiment, participants played two levels of the game. As a result, players continued playing the game after receiving feedback information in order to inform performance on level two. Once participants completed level one and received feedback, they filled out a pencil and paper questionnaire that assessed the dependent variables (with the exception of game performance which was assessed with a measure of actual performance change from level one to level two).

MEASURES

The same measures from the distraction chapter were used in this chapter (attitude toward the game α = .95, perceived relevance α = .81, motivation α = .91. A factor analysis revealed that two items for the attention measure had low factor loadings. After removing those items, the remaining six exhibited high reliability (α = .83). Game performance was also recorded in terms of cash collected and bombs collected.

The same control measures were used as in the distraction chapter. Namely, *gender, age, multitasking ability, game experience,* and *perceived game skill* were assessed.

For the distraction manipulation, at the end of the experiment participants were required to recall the digit string they were asked to memorize. If participants could not accurately recall the digit string then they were eliminated from analysis as this reflected a lack of dedicating cognitive resources to memorization and, ultimately, a lack of manipulation efficacy.

PARTICIPANTS

One hundred five (*N* = 105) participants were recruited from communication courses at a southeastern university. The majority of participants were women (75.70%), Caucasian (75.80%), and between the ages of twenty and twenty-two years old (86.70%), *M* = 21.05, *SD* = 2.76. Participants were randomly assigned and evenly distributed across conditions.

RESULTS

A one-way analysis of variance (ANOVA) revealed a statistically significant effect for the customized feedback manipulation, $F(2, 102) = 40.50, p <.001,$ $\eta_p^2 = .44$. Participants in the customized feedback condition (*M* = 4.75, *SD* = 2.03) perceived the video game feedback to be significantly more "customized" than their counterparts in the non-customized feedback condition (*M* = 2.14, *SD* = 2.04, *p* < .001), and those in the no feedback condition (*M* = 1.98, *SD* = .95, *p* < .001). There was no significant difference between those who received non-customized feedback and those who received no feedback.

In terms of the distraction manipulation, eleven participants were unable to accurately recall the digit string or recorded the digit string on a piece of paper. These participants were eliminated from analysis and were not included among the stated 105 participants.

There was a main effect on attitude, $F(2, 102) = 9.66$, $p < .001$, $\eta_p^2 = .16$. Participants in the customized feedback condition ($M = 3.64$, $SD = 0.92$) had significantly more positive attitudes toward the video game than those in the non-customized feedback condition ($M = 2.85$, $SD = 1.12$, $p < .01$), and those in the no feedback condition ($M = 2.56$, $SD = 1.08$, $p < .01$). There was no significant difference between those who received non-customized feedback and those who received no feedback. There were no significant main effects related to game performance (cash collected and bombs collected).

There were no direct effects of distraction in terms of attitude, cash collected, or bombs collected.

A significant multivariate effect of feedback type was revealed, $F(8, 136) = 4.22$, $p < .001$, Wilks' $\Lambda = .64$, $\eta_p^2 = .20$ but not for distraction. Nor were there significant interaction effects. As for the ANCOVAs associated with this analysis, there were no significant effects for distraction. There were, however, significant differences between feedback type conditions for means of motivation and perceived relevance (table 11.1).

The PROCESS macro (Hayes, 2012) was then used. Model 4 using 2,000 bootstrap samples and 95% CI, was used. Distraction and attention were removed from the analysis since they yielded no significant effects in previous analysis. The indirect effects of feedback type on attitude were significant via motivation (point estimate = .17, Boot SE = .11, CI [.06, .34]), and perceived relevance (point estimate = .18, Boot SE = .08, CI [.04, .36]). Notably, there was no direct effect of feedback type on attitude when accounting for mediators. For game performance, there were no direct effects of the independent variable but there was an indirect effect of feedback type on game performance (bombs collected) via motivation (point estimate = 1.08, Boot SE = .53, CI [.25, 2.38]).

The finding that customized media feedback information enhanced attitudes toward the game is consistent with results from previous customization studies (Ansari & Mela, 2003; Celsi & Olson, 1988; Kalyanaraman & Sundar, 2006; Noar et al., 2011; Rimer & Kreuter, 2006). Customized

Table 11.1 Summary of means and F values for feedback type on potential mediating variables

| Variables | Feedback Type | | | F | η_p^2 |
	No Feedback	Non-Customized	Customized		
Motivation	3.76, 1.45[a]	4.02, 1.25[a]	4.93, 1.19[b]	8.40**	.12
Attention	4.52, .83	4.59, .68	4.76, .71	.81	.02
Perceived	2.05, .91[a]	2.55, .92[a]	3.54, 1.03[b]	19.36**	.30 Relevance

Higher scores indicate more positive perceptions. Comparisons between means, specified by lowercase superscripts, are horizontal only. Cell means that do not share a letter in their superscripts differ at $p < .05$ according to Bonferroni. *$p < .05$. ** $p < .001$.

media feedback information also positively impacted motivation and perceived relevance. The personalized prizes presented to participants in the customized media feedback condition presumably prompted greater motivation to succeed in the game because the personalized prizes were *exactly* what the participants desired. In a similar vein, customization is an effective strategy for generating perceived relevance for users who are playing a new game.

Accordingly, the effect of feedback type on attitude was fully mediated by motivation and relevance. In other words, customized media feedback resulted in more positive attitudes toward the game because players felt more motivated and perceived the game to be more relevant to them. In terms of game performance, customized feedback had a positive impact on motivation, and increased motivation led to more improved performance in the game as related to bombs collected but not cash collected. Essentially, when people were more motivated to play well, they did, and customized feedback served as a source of motivation. Most of the participants were not likely interested in playing the game but by making the feedback customized to them, they became more interested.

While these findings help illuminate how media feedback functions and the importance of relevance, the lack of significant results related to distraction is particularly puzzling, especially in conjunction with the distractions chapter. Perhaps the customization manipulation subsumed the effects of distraction. That is, the effects of distraction dissipated when the customization manipulation was used. This would provide a stronger argument for the power of customization. However, there is also the chance that these findings were spurious and should be interpreted with caution.

The purpose of this chapter was to introduce a possible explanation of media feedback efficacy via relevance by examining the nuances of customized media feedback. Perhaps the most central finding in this chapter was that customized feedback was superior to other forms of feedback. Customized feedback improved performance and invoked more positive attitudes compared to non-customized feedback and no feedback. Although the importance of individualized content within feedback has been vaguely alluded to in the literature (Glanz et al. 2010; Hattie & Timperley, 2007; Hawkins et al., 2008; Kluger & DeNisi, 1996), this assumption has not received much empirical examination until now. This study indicates that the self plays a central role in media feedback (Baumeister, 1998). This finding, hopefully, will usher in new strategies for administering media feedback as this shows some of the central mechanisms that underpin effective media feedback.

Distractions had no impact on attitude. In the distractions chapter, when the effects of distractions were manifested, they were unexpected. Distractions actually enhanced game performance through decreased attention, contrary to predictions based on existing literature (Drolet & Luce, 2004; Lamble et al., 1999; Ward & Mann, 2000). This finding should be taken with caution as this was likely a unique scenario wherein distraction did not behave as typically predicted in media feedback.

Another contribution of this chapter was the further parsing of the approach/avoidance paradigm by testing the behaviors of collecting money and avoiding bombs. As noted, feedback has been divided based on approach (sometimes mislabeled as positive) and avoid (sometimes mislabeled as negative) performance evaluations (Carnagey & Anderson, 2005; Carver & Scheier, 2001; Hattie & Timperlay, 2007; Ramaprasad, 1983; Reinecke et al., 2012) but this indicates that instructions/descriptions of behaviors before the feedback loop had started have not been afforded enough consideration. This chapter and the distractions chapter provide evidence that effects on performance vary based on whether a behavior was described as approaching a positive outcome or avoiding a negative outcome. Improvement on approach behaviors was predicted by different factors than improvement on avoid behaviors. In turn, these chapters offer a theoretical contribution regarding conceptualization and operationalization of performance behaviors as approach/avoid and "positive/negative" as well as another systematic explanation for inconsistencies in feedback studies. These findings should inform industry practices in terms of feedback design and implementation.

Chapter 12

Veracity of Media Feedback

Many of the preceding chapters have dealt with the traits of and key concepts related to media feedback. As a review, the book has covered implicit versus explicit media feedback, approach and avoid feedback, positive and negative feedback as well as the timeliness, frequency, relevance, and authority of media feedback. Each of these chapters has argued that certain attributes are important to effective media feedback. However, when dealing with users, much of the efficacy is gleaned from user perceptions of the feedback. In other words, the *actual* traits of feedback may not be as important as how the users feel about the feedback.

This naturally leads to skepticism regarding whether or not feedback needs these traits or just needs to make the user *think* that the feedback has these traits. Indeed, do any of the traits matter if efficacy is all a matter of perception? This chapter is dedicated to exploring whether or not the veracity of media feedback (whether it is true/accurate or false/inaccurate) has any bearing on user perceptions of media feedback.

This area of inquiry is of particular importance because many studies use false feedback as a manipulation—several of the previous chapters did so. Perhaps one of the most famous examples of this is the bogus pipeline (Jones & Sighall, 1971). The bogus pipeline was not designed to test the perceptions of the veracity of feedback, but the conceptual backbone of the bogus pipeline and veracity of feedback are similar. The bogus pipeline was developed in order to elicit truthful responses from participants. This was particularly applicable when researchers were looking at sensitive topics where participants might give false responses in order to save themselves embarrassment or acquire social desirability. For example, if a researcher was interested in studying racism, sexism, or illegal drug use, the participant might be inclined to lie during the study in order to appear less racist or sexist, and more law-abiding than he or she might truthfully be.

When using the bogus pipeline, participants are told that they are being attached to a lie detector even though the researcher is not actually using a lie detector. Since participants perceive that their responses to sensitive questions are exposed as true or false, then participants tend to be more truthful than if they are not attached to the bogus pipeline. To frame this another way, the participants *think* they have entered a feedback loop wherein the accuracy of their answers is measured by a lie detector. The lie detector itself is inconsequential, the perception of the lie detector is what is salient.

In the same way, the media feedback platform may be inconsequential, just user perceptions of it a matter. The examples here can become convoluted but for starters, if a person takes an online quiz and has no idea what the answers are, then the feedback loop is inconsequential because the person has no frame of reference for whether or not the feedback is accurate. In a video game, this may be even more appropriate such that players might be given multiple quests that funnel them in multiple directions even if only one is the most optimal path for goal completion

For another example, users may see advertisements on their Twitter feed that they may not recognize as advertisements. The advertisements have reached the users because of a feedback loop that has targeted the users. In this case, the users are never aware of the feedback loop and thus the status of the advertisements as advertisements is not important, only the users' perception of the advertisement. The same logic can be applied to native advertising and social influencers who endorse products as if they are just a typical social media user. A person could see an individual whom he or she follows on Instagram saying that a shampoo has worked great for them but in reality, this individual has never used the shampoo and is being paid to endorse it. Again, the perception of a feedback loop is being manipulated to provide false information.

Unless the user recognizes the information as false or is unaware that he or she has entered a feedback loop, the veracity of feedback should not matter to users. Thus, many of the traits of effective feedback and how it is understood can be challenged as, to use an old adage, perception is reality.

METHOD

In this study, a 2-condition experiment was used. Participants took an online quiz, similar to the one used in chapter four. In one condition, participants received true or accurate feedback and in the other condition participants received false or inaccurate feedback. In the true or accurate feedback condition, participants were told if they got the answer correct or incorrect, accurately. In the false or inaccurate feedback condition, participants were told they got the answer correct if they were incorrect or incorrect if they were correct.

From there, participants were asked to fill out a questionnaire detailing their attitudes and perceptions specific to their condition.

Measures

Each of the measures indicated acceptable reliability (competence $\alpha = .91$, autonomy $\alpha = .84$, relatedness $\alpha = .96$, surveillance $\alpha = .95$, cognitive load $\alpha = .73$, information comprehensibility $\alpha = .74$, information comprehensiveness $\alpha = .94$). For information accuracy, the item, "The information is not precise" was removed and the remaining two items were correlated, $r = .75$ $p < .01$. $\alpha = .93$. For relevance, the item, "The information does not help me at all." was removed and the remaining two items were correlated, $r = .48$, $p < .01$. The sample was also asked about how often they participated in trivia/quizzes.

Participants

After removing participants who failed the attention checks, 181 remained. The participants were majority white (66.9%) males (53.0%) in their late-30s ($M = 37.35$), and 54.7 percent made $69,999 or less. The sample on average played trivia and quizzes on average of 512.51 ($SD = 64.27$) per month. Notably, this group participated in trivia and quizzes far more often than those in the positive and negative feedback chapter (chapter four).

RESULTS

Feelings of enjoyment, discouragement, encouragement, entertainment, meaningfulness, competence, autonomy, relatedness, information accuracy, cognitive load, surveillance, information comprehensibility, information comprehensiveness, frequency, and information relevance were entered as dependent variables. The condition, feedback veracity, was used as the independent variable. Age, gender, race, income, and how often trivia is played were entered as covariates. This analysis revealed multivariate effect of feedback veracity exactly on the threshold of significance ($F(14, 159) = 4.11$, $p = .05$, Wilks' $\Lambda = .73$, $\eta_p 2 = .27$).

The individual ANOVAs related to feedback veracity significantly impacted feelings of enjoyment ($F(1, 172) = 4.71$, $p < .05$, $\eta_p 2 = .03$), "true" feedback $M = 4.48$, $SD = 1.96$, "false" feedback $M = 5.07$, $SD = 1.69$), encouragement ($F(1, 172) = 6.70$ $p < .01$, $\eta_p2 = .04$), "true" feedback $M = 3.13$, $SD = 1.93$, "false" feedback $M = 3.86$, $SD = 1.89$), competence ($F(1, 172) = 17.09$, $p < .001$, $\eta_p2 = .09$), "true" feedback $M = 3.51$, $SD = 1.93$, "false" feedback $M = 4.67$, $SD = 1.66$), autonomy ($F(1, 172) = 11.10$, $p < .01$, $\eta_p2 = .06$), "true" feedback $M = 4.25$, $SD = 1.65$, "false" feedback $M = 4.96$, $SD = 1.32$), relatedness ($F(1, 172) = 4.84$, $p < .05$, $\eta_p2 = .03$), "true" feedback $M = 2.84$, $SD = 1.92$, "false" feedback $M = 3.49$, $SD = 2.11$).

In order to fully test mediation, the PROCESS macro (Hayes, 2018) was used.

Competence, autonomy, relatedness, and encouragement were entered as mediators. Enjoyment was entered as the outcome variable. The condition was entered as the independent variable. Age, gender, race, income, and how often the participant played trivia were entered as covariates. Model 4 using 2,000 bootstrap samples and 95 percent CI, was employed. The direct effect of the condition dissipated but there were indirect effects on enjoyment via autonomy (point estimate = .29, Boot SE = .12, CI [.08, .57.]) and encouragement (point estimate = .21, Boot SE = .10, CI [.04, .44]).

The prescribed hierarchical regression was used. In step 1, age, gender, race, income, time spent playing trivia were entered. In step 2, feelings of discouragement, encouragement, competence, autonomy, relatedness, information accuracy, cognitive load, surveillance, information comprehensibility, information comprehensiveness, and information relevance were entered. In step 3, the condition was entered. Enjoyment was entered as the dependent variable. These results are detailed in table 12.1. This was run twice more with meaningfulness entered as the dependent variable and entertainment entered as the dependent variable (table 12.2 and 12.3).

As noted, the results from the front end of this analysis are on the threshold of significance. Likewise, the sample reported an inordinate amount of participation in trivia and quizzes. The frontend results should be viewed through this lens.

While media feedback veracity had significant effects on enjoyment, encouragement, autonomy, competence, and relatedness, all of these means were higher for false feedback than for true feedback. The quiz was deliberately designed to be challenging. Since the quiz was challenging, those receiving true feedback were often being told that they were incorrect while those receiving false feedback were often told that they were correct. This would explain why the false feedback condition engendered greater feelings of enjoyment, encouragement, autonomy, competence, and relatedness. This does indicate show that users' perceptions of feedback override the impact of the veracity of feedback. The feedback loop was more effective when it was false than when it was true. This provides some evidence that veracity in media feedback can be manipulated in all sorts of ways in order

Table 12.1 Regression Analysis for Enjoyment

	B	SE	β
Step 1			
Gender	-.33	.28	-.09
Age	.00	.01	-.03
Race`	-.05	.08	-.05
Income	.04	.04	.07
Play Trivia	.00	.00	-.06
	$F(5, 178) = .55$		
	Adj. $R^2 = -.02$		
Step 2			
Gender	.14	.20	.04
Age	.00	.01	.00
Race`	-.07	.05	-.06
Income	.02	.03	.04
Play Trivia	.00	.00	-.05
Discouraging	-.26	.06	-.29[c]
Encouraging	.23	.07	.24[b]
Frequent	.01	.06	.01
Competence	.13	.07	.13
Autonomy	.29	.08	.24[c]
Relatedness	.12	.08	.13
Cognitive Load	.10	.11	.06
Surveillance	-.04	.09	-.04
Information Accuracy	.10	.10	.08
Information Comprehensibility	.18	.11	.12
Information Comprehensiveness	-.05	.09	-.04
Relevance	.20	.10	.15
	$F(12, 178) = 13.62$[c]		
	Adj. $R^2 = .55$		
Step 3			
Gender	.14	.20	.04
Age	.00	.01	.00
Race`	-.07	.05	-.06
Income	.02	.03	.04
Play Trivia	.00	.00	-.05
Discouraging	.27	.06	.20[c]
Encouraging	.23	.07	.24[b]
Frequent	.01	.06	.01
Competence	.13	.07	.13
Autonomy	.30	.08	.25[c]
Relatedness	.12	.09	.13
Cognitive Load	.09	.11	.06
Surveillance	-.08	.09	-.04
Information Accuracy	.08	.11	.07
Information Comprehensibility	.18	.11	.12
Information Comprehensiveness	-.04	.09	-.03
Relevance	.21	.10	.15[a]
Veracity	-.11	.22	-.03
	$F(1, 178) = 12.82$[c]		
	Adj. $R^2 = .54$		

[a]$p < 0.05$. [b]$p < 0.01$, [c]$p < 0.001$. No superscript $p > 0.05$

Table 12.2   Regression Analysis for Meaningfulness

	B	SE	β
Step 1			
Gender	-.59	.30	-.15[a]
Age	-.02	.01	-.12
Race`	.08	.08	.07
Income	.01	.05	.02
Play Trivia	.00	.00	-.08
	$F(5, 178) = 1.62$		
	Adj. $R^2 = -.02$		
Step 2			
Gender	.25	.20	.06
Age	.00	.01	-.02
Race`	.04	.05	.04
Income	-.02	.03	-.03
Play Trivia	.00	.00	-.04
Discouraging	-.13	.06	-.13[a]
Encouraging	.38	.07	.36[c]
Frequent	.02	.06	.02
Competence	.07	.07	.07
Autonomy	.15	.08	.11
Relatedness	.24	.08	.25[b]
Cognitive Load	.24	.11	.15[a]
Surveillance	.20	.09	.19[a]
Information Accuracy	-.16	.10	-.11[a]
Information Comprehensibility	.24	.11	.14[a]
Information Comprehensiveness	-.10	.09	-.08
Relevance	.14	.10	.09
	$F(12, 178) = 18.38^c$		
	Adj. $R^2 = .62$		
Step 3			
Gender	.24	.20	.06
Age	.00	.01	.01
Race`	.04	.05	.04
Income	.02	.03	.04
Play Trivia	.00	.00	-.04
Discouraging	-.14	.06	-.14[a]
Encouraging	.39	.07	.37[c]
Frequent	.02	.06	.02
Competence	.09	.07	.08
Autonomy	.17	.08	.13[a]
Relatedness	.25	.08	.25[b]
Cognitive Load	.23	.11	.14[a]
Surveillance	.21	.08	.20[a]
Information Accuracy	-.22	.11	-.16[a]
Information Comprehensibility	.23	.11	.14[a]
Information Comprehensiveness	-.08	.09	-.06
Relevance	.16	.10	.10
Veracity	-.34	.22	-.08
	$F(1, 178) = 17.64^c$		
	Adj. $R^2 = .63$		

[a] $p < 0.05$. [b] $p < 0.01$, [c] $p < 0.001$. No superscript $p > 0.05$

Table 12.3   Regression Analysis for Entertainment

	B	SE	β
Step 1			
Gender	-.33	.28	-.09
Age	.00	.01	-.03
Race`	-.05	.08	-.05
Income	.04	.04	.07
Play Trivia	.00	.00	-.06
	$F(5, 178) = .67$		
	Adj. $R^2 = -.01$		
Step 2			
Gender	.00	.21	.00
Age	.01	.01	.05
Race`	.01	.06	.01
Income	.01	.03	.02
Play Trivia	.00	.00	-.02
Discouraging	-.23	.06	-.25[b]
Encouraging	.24	.08	.25[b]
Frequent	.07	.06	.07
Competence	.06	.08	.06
Autonomy	.23	.09	.19[b]
Relatedness	.16	.09	.18
Cognitive Load	.06	.12	.04
Surveillance	.01	.09	.01
Information Accuracy	.07	.10	.06
Information Comprehensibility	.28	.11	.19[a]
Information Comprehensiveness	-.08	.10	-.07
Relevance	.10	.11	.07
	$F(12, 178) = 10.61$[c]		
	Adj. $R^2 = .48$		
Step 3			
Gender	-.01	.21	.00
Age	.01	.01	.06
Race`	-.01	.06	-.01
Income	.01	.03	.01
Play Trivia	.00	.00	-.01
Discouraging	.23	.06	.26[c]
Encouraging	.25	.08	.27[c]
Frequent	.07	.06	.07
Competence	.07	.08	.08
Autonomy	.24	.09	.20[b]
Relatedness	.16	.09	.18
Cognitive Load	.05	.12	.04
Surveillance	.02	.09	.02
Information Accuracy	.02	.11	.01
Information Comprehensibility	.28	.11	.19[a]
Information Comprehensiveness	-.06	.10	-.05
Relevance	.11	.11	.08
Veracity	-.30	.23	-.08
	$F(1, 178) = 10.16$[c]		
	Adj. $R^2 = .48$		

[a]$p < 0.05$. [b]$p < 0.01$, [c]$p < 0.001$. No superscript $p > 0.05$

to alter user perception and that perception will be based on factors other than the feedback loop itself. The results here should not be understated and suggest that perception can very well be reality when it comes to media feedback.

While using the PROCESS macro, the effect of veracity was subsumed by feelings of autonomy and encouragement such that individuals felt more autonomy and encouragement from false feedback which led to greater feelings of enjoyment.

In terms of the regression, enjoyment was positively predicted by encouragement, autonomy, and relevance, but negatively by discouragement. Entertainment was positively predicted by encouragement, autonomy, and information comprehensibility, but negatively by discouragement. Meaningfulness was positively predicted by encouragement, autonomy, cognitive load, surveillance, and information comprehensibility, but negatively by discouragement and information accuracy.

Most of these results are expected with the exception of how information accuracy and cognitive load predicted meaningfulness. Higher cognitive load may predict more meaningfulness because it presented a challenge and thus was more engaging. Also, the questions were about people so deeper engagement could relate to feelings of connection with others. As for information accuracy, this finding is appropriate given the topic of this chapter. In this chapter, accuracy did not matter all that much for media feedback though this particular finding is unclear and should be explored further.

Chapter 13

User Media Feedback and System Media Feedback

Thus far, this book has mainly covered system generated feedback loops as opposed to user generated feedback loops. Historically, media feedback has typically been between the user and a system (using a computer without internet). With the development of Web 2.0 this has shifted so feedback information can come from other users instead of the system. This is often referred to as computer-mediated communications or CMC.

Now, many of the most popular media platforms in the current media environment connect users socially and promote CMC. As a result, many of these platforms provide feedback loops that are both system produced and produced by other users. For example, review aggregator sites such as *Rotten Tomatoes* or *Metacritic* offer an official score for entertainment properties that the site has curated and present to users—not to mention the host of other feedback loops on the sites like navigating the site, clicking buttons, reading articles, and encountering advertisements targeted at users based on their past behaviors. However, these sites also allow users to post their own reviews. In turn, there is system feedback information for the user to consume as well as less formal, "unofficial" reviews from other site users. Both provide feedback information but are likely viewed in different ways since one is from the system and the other is from other users. One might be more likely to trust the system, or one might be more likely to trust other users.

Sundar provides a compelling dissection of this dichotomy (2008, p. 83).

It is commonplace for us to say that we got something "off the computer." In this case, the psychologically relevant agent is the computer itself. . . . If an interface appears machine-like, then it may cue the machine heuristic, resulting in attributions of randomness, objectivity, and other mechanical

characteristics to its performance. This may indeed result in positive credibility judgments.

In contrast, is the bandwagon heuristic—if others find a product favorable
then others should find it favorable too. There is evidence that the source
of content, from the system or from other users impacts the perceptions of
people consuming content (Sundar & Nass, 2001). Sundar, Oeldorf-Hirsch,
and Xu (2008) showed that the bandwagon heuristic influences opinions and
the user's behavior.

While there is a degree of research in this area, this chapter bridges this
existing body of research to media feedback. When someone is looking for
the best articles to read or the best products to buy, he or she is effectively
entering a feedback loop as determined by either the media platform or
people who use the media platform. This naturally adds to the conversation
on implicit versus explicit feedback as one might interpret system generated
or user generated feedback as either implicit or explicit, but arguments could
be made in either direction. For example, system generated feedback information might convey an explicit "buy this" message or it might be providing
a subtle hint to the user. On the other hand, user generated feedback information could be presented as explicit as one user might say "do not buy this
product," whereas the number of user ratings on a product could be seen as
implicit feedback. This is not an original concept. Knobloch-Westerwick and
colleagues (2005) used explicit (average rating) or implicit (times viewed)
user recommendations in a study and the results indicated that the explicit
recommendations had a greater effect on participants while implicit feedback
had a curvilinear effect.

METHOD

For this study, a 2-condition experiment was used to address the impact of
system generated feedback information versus user generated feedback information on a media platform. Participants were randomly assigned to a condition. In the system generated feedback information condition, participants
were presented with a set of "suggested" products from Amazon.com based
on their browsing and viewing history. In the user generated feedback information condition, participants were presented with the same set of products
from Amazon.com but were presented with user reviews in the form of star
ratings instead of suggested products.

From there, participants were asked to fill out a questionnaire detailing
their attitudes and perceptions specific to their condition.

Measures

Each of the measures indicated acceptable reliability (competence $\alpha = .95$, autonomy $\alpha = .88$, relatedness $\alpha = .93$, surveillance $\alpha = .86$, cognitive load $\alpha = .85$, information comprehensiveness $\alpha = .91$). For information accuracy, the item, "The information is not precise" was removed and the remaining two items were correlated, $r = .80$, $p < .01$. For information comprehensibility, the item, "The information is not presented in an adequate way" was removed and the remaining three items were related, $\alpha = .93$. For relevance, the item, "The information does not help me at all." was removed and the remaining two items were correlated, $r = .74$, $p < .01$. Participants were also asked how often they use Amazon, how much they like Amazon, and how likely they would be to purchase one of the products displayed

Participants

After removing participants who failed the attention checks, 178 remained. The participants were majority white (77.5%) males (53.9%) in their early-40s ($M = 41.92$), and 53.2 percent made $59,999 or less. The sample on average used Amazon for purchases 8.26 times a month of ($SD = 17.33$) and liked Amazon for an average of 5.72 ($SD = 1.45$) on a scale from 1–7.

RESULTS

Feelings of enjoyment, discouragement, encouragement, entertainment, meaningfulness, competence, autonomy, relatedness, information accuracy, cognitive load, surveillance, information comprehensibility, information comprehensiveness, frequency, likelihood of making a purchase, and information relevance were entered as dependent variables. User or system generated feedback information was used as the independent variable. Age, gender, race, income, how often Amazon is used, and how much Amazon is liked were entered as covariates. This analysis revealed a multivariate effect of feedback frequency that approached significance ($F(16, 144) = 1.74$, $p = .05$, Wilks' $\Lambda = .84$, $\eta_p2 = .16$) and the only significant ANOVA was for autonomy ($F(1, 159) = 6.32$, $p < .05$, $\eta_p2 = .04$), user generated feedback information $M = 5.15$, $SD = 1.48$, system generated feedback information $M = 5.45$, $SD = 1.11$).

To interpret this rather tenuous finding, people felt more freedom when they saw system generated feedback information. This is compelling because it adds an unexpected dimension to what previous literature suggests regarding the bandwagon heuristic. However, the concept of autonomy may be tapping into a specific set of psychological factors. While feelings of autonomy generally are perceived to enhance positive feelings toward content, autonomy was likely depleted when looking at user generated feedback information, one might have felt like others were asserting their will upon his or her decisions. Meanwhile, the system generated feedback information might have felt like the system was pushing one toward a decision, but that decision was based on previous behavior. Thus, the participant's previous autonomous choices led to this content, not simply user reviews.

Given these weak results, the PROCESS macro was forgone, and the prescribed hierarchical regression was used. In step 1, age, gender, race, income, how often Amazon is used, and how much Amazon is liked were entered. In step 2, feelings of discouragement, encouragement, frequency, likelihood of purchase, competence, autonomy, relatedness, information accuracy, cognitive load, surveillance, information comprehensibility, information comprehensiveness, and information relevance were entered. In step 3, the condition was entered. Enjoyment was entered as the dependent variable. These results are detailed in table 13.1. This was run twice more with meaningfulness entered as the dependent variable and entertainment entered as the dependent variable (table 13.2 and 13.3).

In the first model, enjoyment was predicted by how much participants liked Amazon, how autonomous and related to others it made them feel. Also, enjoyment was predicted by lower feelings of discouragement and greater feelings of encouragement. These findings are noteworthy as this scenario was one that is highly generalizable compared to some of the other studies in this book.

The second model showed that feelings of meaningfulness were predicted by age and income such that certain ages and people who made less money were more likely to find meaningful experiences on Amazon. Feelings of meaningfulness were also predicted by relatedness and information accuracy but there was a negative relationship with information accuracy. The more accurate the information felt, the less meaningful it was. Perhaps this is because meaningfulness is a broadening and opening to other human experiences. As a result, when information was too accurate, it reduced some of the mystery of the human condition and led to lower feelings of meaningfulness.

In the third and final model, entertainment was predicted by lower feelings of discouragement but greater feelings of encouragement, relatedness, surveillance, information comprehensibility. None of these findings are particularly surprising. The upshot from this chapter should be that there is a difference between system generated feedback information and user generated feedback information even though the results were not particularly strong.

Table 13.1 Regression Analysis for Enjoyment

	B	SE	β
Step 1			
Gender	.42	.23	.13
Age	.00	.01	-.01
Race	.10	.09	.08
Income	-.01	.03	-.03
Use Amazon	.00	.01	.04
Like Amazon	.48	.08	.42[c]
	$F_{(6, 166)} = 7.66^c$		
	Adj. $R^2 = .19$		
Step 2			
Gender	.23	.13	.07
Age	.00	.00	.02
Race	.04	.05	.03
Income	-.02	.02	-.05
Use Amazon	.00	.00	.03
Like Amazon	.14	.05	.13[b]
Discouraging	-.15	.04	-.16[b]
Encouraging	.15	.06	.17[b]
Frequency	.11	.07	.11
Purchase.12	.06	.13	
Competence	.02	.08	.02
Autonomy	.17	.09	.14
Relatedness	.15	.06	.15[a]
Cognitive Load	.00	.07	.00
Surveillance	.04	.08	.04
Information Accuracy	.13	.09	.10
Information Comprehensibility	.11	.09	.08
Information Comprehensiveness	-.12	.09	-.10
Relevance	.19	.10	.16
	$F_{(13, 166)} = 28.46^c$		
	Adj. $R^2 = .75$		
Step 3			
Gender	.23	.13	.07
Age	.00	.00	-.03
Race	.05	.05	.04
Income	-.03	.02	-.06
Use Amazon	.00	.00	.04
Like Amazon	.14	.05	.12[b]
Discouraging	-.15	.04	-.17[b]
Encouraging	.16	.06	.18[b]
Frequency	.11	.07	.11
Purchase	.13	.06	.14
Competence	.05	.08	.04
Autonomy	.18	.09	.15[a]
Relatedness	.15	.06	.15[a]
Cognitive Load	.00	.07	.00

(Continued)

Table 13.1   Regression Analysis for Enjoyment (*Continued*)

	B	SE	β
Surveillance	.04	.08	.04
Information Accuracy	.12	.09	.09
Information Comprehensibility	.11	.09	.08
Information Comprehensiveness	-.12	.09	-.09
Relevance	.19	.10	.16
Condition	.10	.14	.03
	$F(1, 166) = 27.00^c$		
	Adj. $R^2 = .75$		

[a]$p < 0.05.$ [b]$p < 0.01,$ [c]$p < 0.001.$ No superscript $p > 0.05.$

Table 13.2 Regression Analysis for Meaningfulness

	B	SE	β
Step 1			
Gender	.11	.28	.03
Age	.00	.01	.04
Race`	.10	.10	.07
Income	-.07	.04	-.13
Use Amazon	.01	.01	.10
Like Amazon	.27	.10	.22[b]
	$F(6, 166) = 2.22$[a]		
	Adj. $R^2 = .04$		
Step 2			
Gender	.12	.17	.03
Age	.01	.01	.10[a]
Race`	.02	.06	.01
Income	-.05	.03	-.10[a]
Use Amazon	.01	.00	.07
Like Amazon	-.07	.07	-.05
Discouraging	-.08	.06	-.08
Encouraging	.30	.08	.30[c]
Frequency	.14	.09	.12
Purchase	.16	.08	.16
Competence	-.03	.11	-.02
Autonomy	.09	.12	.06
Relatedness	.20	.07	.19[b]
Cognitive Load	.12	.09	.09
Surveillance	.09	.10	.08
Information Accuracy	-.30	.12	-.21[a]
Information Comprehensibility	.04	.12	.03
Information Comprehensiveness	.20	.11	.15
Relevance	.16	13	.12
	$F(13, 166) = 17.60$[c]		
	Adj. $R^2 = .65$		
Step 3			
Gender	.11	.17	.03
Age	.01	.01	.10
Race`	.02	.07	.01
Income	-.06	.03	-.11[a]
Use Amazon	.01	.00	.07
Like Amazon	-.07	.07	-.05
Discouraging	-.08	.06	-.08
Encouraging	.29	.08	.30[c]
Frequency	.14	.09	.12
Purchase	.16	.08	.16
Competence	-.03	.11	-.02
Autonomy	.09	.12	.07
Relatedness	.20	.07	.19[b]
Cognitive Load	.12	.09	.09

(Continued)

Chapter 13

Table 13.2 Regression Analysis for Meaningfulness (*Continued*)

	B	SE	β
Surveillance	.09	.10	.08
Information Accuracy	-.30	.12	-.22[a]
Information Comprehensibility	.04	.12	.02
Information Comprehensiveness	.21	.11	.15
Relevance	.16	.13	.12
Condition	.03	.18	.01
	$F(1, 166) = 16.61$[c]		
	Adj. R^2 = .65		

[a]$p < 0.05$. [b]$p < 0.01$, [c]$p < 0.001$. No superscript $p > 0.05$.

Table 13.3   Regression Analysis for Entertainment

	B	SE	β
Step 1			
Gender	.38	.25	.11
Age	.00	.01	.01
Race`	.10	.10	.08
Income	-.01	.04	-.02
Use Amazon	.00	.01	.02
Like Amazon	.40	.09	.34[c]
	$F(6, 166) = 4.60^c$		
	Adj. $R^2 = .11$		
Step 2			
Gender	.22	.16	.06
Age	.00	.01	.00
Race`	.06	.06	.05
Income	-.01	.02	-.03
Use Amazon	.00	.00	.02
Like Amazon	.06	.06	.05
Discouraging	-.13	.05	-.14[a]
Encouraging	.31	.07	.34[c]
Frequency	-.05	.08	-.05
Purchase	.12	.08	.13
Competence	.09	.10	.07
Autonomy	.15	.11	.12
Relatedness	.18	.07	.18[b]
Cognitive Load	.02	.08	.02
Surveillance	.22	.09	.20[a]
Information Accuracy	-.17	.11	-.13
Information Comprehensibility	.33	.11	.22[b]
Information Comprehensiveness	-.19	.10	-.14
Relevance	.08	.12	.06
	$F(13, 166) = 18.98^c$		
	Adj. $R^2 = .66$		
Step 3			
Gender	.21	.16	.06
Age	.00	.01	.00
Race`	.06	.06	.05
Income	-.02	.02	-.03
Use Amazon	.00	.00	.02
Like Amazon	.06	.06	.05
Discouraging	-.13	.05	-.14[a]
Encouraging	.30	.07	.33[c]
Frequency	-.05	.08	-.05
Purchase	.12	.08	.13
Competence	.09	.10	.07
Autonomy	.16	.11	.13
Relatedness	.19	.07	.19[b]
Cognitive Load	.02	.08	.02

(Continued)

Table 13.3   Regression Analysis for Entertainment (*Continued*)

	B	SE	β
Surveillance	.24	.10	.22[b]
Information Accuracy	-.18	.11	-.13
Information Comprehensibility	.32	.11	.22[b]
Information Comprehensiveness	-.18	.10	-.14
Relevance	.08	.12	.06
Condition.	10	.17	.03
$F(1, 166) = 17.89^c$			
Adj. $R^2 = .66$			

[a]$p < 0.05$. [b]$p < 0.01$, [c]$p < 0.001$. No superscript $p > 0.05$.

Chapter 14

Media Feedback from Users

The previous chapter compared user generated feedback information versus system generated feedback information. This chapter aims to look a bit deeper at user generated feedback as it is so prominent in the current media landscape. When someone posts something online, that content is often open to comments and some sort of rating system. Facebook allows for likes, emotes, and comments. Twitter allows for likes, retweets, and comments. Instagram allows for comments and likes while measuring the number of views a post receives. Reddit has a comments section as well as an up vote/down vote system for content posted. At the time of writing this chapter, seven of the top ten websites trafficked (according to Alexa.com) allowed for users to provide some direct form of feedback information on the page.

This ability to provide to and solicit feedback information from so many so quickly and removing barriers for those who may not be able to participate in discussions otherwise has been heralded as a boon for democracy (Finley, 2017). Certainly, providing voices to individuals is a noteworthy endeavor but this also opens users to a darker side of media feedback. An anecdote of self-satire may best illustrate this principle. The Federal Communications Commission (FCC) solicited feedback information from individuals on the topic of Net Neutrality, a movement dedicated to removing the power of internet service providers to alter internet services to individual users based on a number of factors. "[I]n opening its virtual doors to the public, it's also opened them to spammers and trolls, some of whom might have even managed to knock the FCC's site offline" (Finley, 2017). This shows "just how hard it is to turn the web into a platform for democratic participation. Just look at any comments section on the internet" (Finley, 2017). That comment, "Just look at any comments section on the internet," is not expanded upon at all, assuming readers will know its implication being that feedback information on websites tends to be brimming with "spammers and trolls" or other detractors. The FCC essentially created a feedback loop that quickly spiraled out of its control because of how users were participating in the loop.

In sum, media feedback from users can be empowering but it can also allow for antisocial behaviors. This creates a precarious situation for content creators who are creating feedback loops. Content creators could be praised, maligned, or subjected to outright malice. As a result, content creators may be putting themselves in a relatively vulnerable position psychologically.

In two studies, Burrow and Rainone (2017) argued how important "likes" on social media were to self-esteem. In the first study, a survey showed that self-esteem was positively predicted by the number of likes received on social media. In the second study, the researchers used an experiment where the number of likes received was manipulated and the results were similar to study one. These results are not unique (Brooks, 2015; Valkenburg, Peter, & Schouten, 2006).

Another study performed a survey regarding social media and psychological well-being (Sabik, Falat, & Magagnos, 2019). In this study, a survey demonstrated that the importance a user put on media feedback information was associated with status-seeking on social media while status-seeking was associated with stress, depression, and frequent social media use. Importantly, this study also argued that there is a large gap in this area of research related to feedback. The chapter hopes to help fill some of that gap.

Social media sites are capable of providing a large volume of feedback information. Consider the difference between showing an individual a photograph in person versus broadcasting it online to a wide audience. Instead of one point of feedback information, the photograph can receive virtually limitless feedback information. When a teacher grades a paper, that is only one feedback source. If that paper were graded online by multiple teachers, there would be many sources of feedback information. This is likely contributing to the psychological impact of media feedback. This chapter looks at the volume of feedback information a user receives.

METHOD

A 3-condition experiment was used to test the impact volume of feedback information from users. Participants were randomly assigned to a condition. The method was adapted from the experiment used by Burrow and Rainone (2017) such that participants were told that they received a certain amount of likes on a post they had made to social media. The low likes condition received one like on their post. The medium likes condition received thirty-seven likes on their post. The high likes condition received 699 likes on their post. These figures were determined by a pretest asking people what they would consider low, medium, and high number of likes on one of their posts. Please note that the participants' actual social media accounts were not used in this study.

Measures

Each of the measures indicated acceptable reliability (competence $\alpha = .95$, autonomy $\alpha = .90$, relatedness $\alpha = .93$, surveillance $\alpha = .95$, cognitive load $\alpha = .83$, information comprehensibility $\alpha = .69$, information comprehensiveness $\alpha = .93$, relevance $\alpha = .72$). For information accuracy, the item, "The information is not precise" was removed and the remaining two items were correlated, $r = .70$ $p < .01$. In addition to these items, participants were asked how much they like social media, how often they use social media, how often they post on social media, and how many likes they get on an average post.

Participants

After removing participants who failed the attention checks, 296 remained. The participants were majority white (68.0%) females (50.7%) in their late-30s ($M = 37.19$), and 56.9 percent made \$69,999 or less. The sample on average used social media 8.04 times a day, posted on social media on average of 6.92 times a month, liked social media on average of 5.27 on a scale of 1-7, and received an average of 113.49 likes on their posts though this figure was skewed by a handful of outliers.

RESULTS

Feelings of enjoyment, discouragement, encouragement, entertainment, meaningfulness, competence, autonomy, relatedness, information accuracy, cognitive load, surveillance, information comprehensibility, information comprehensiveness, frequency, and information relevance were entered as dependent variables. The condition was used as the independent variable. Age, gender, race, income, use of social media, posting on social media, liking social media, and likes on posts were entered as covariates. This analysis revealed a significant multivariate effect of media feedback from users ($F(28, 540) = 6.78$, $p = .001$, Wilks' $\Lambda = .55$, $\eta_p 2 = .26$).

The individual ANOVAs showed that media feedback from users significantly impacted feelings of enjoyment ($F(2, 283) = 49.21$, $p < .001$, $\eta_p 2 = .26$), entertainment ($F(2, 283) = 54.37$, $p < .001$, $\eta_p 2 = .28$), meaningfulness

$(F(2, 283) = 19.98, p < .001, \eta_p2 = .12)$, discouragement $(F(2, 283) = 11.16,$ $p < .001, \eta_p2 = .07)$, encouragement $(F(2, 283) = 56.15, p < .001, \eta_p2 = .28)$, frequency $(F(2, 283) = 53.46, p < .001, \eta_p2 = .27)$, competence $(F(2, 283) = 37.57, p < .001, \eta_p2 = .21)$, autonomy $(F(2, 283) = 14.55, p < .001, \eta_p2 = .09)$, relatedness $(F(2, 283) = 46.10, p < .001, \eta_p2 = .25)$, surveillance $(F(2, 283) = 26.23, p < .001, \eta_p2 = .16)$, information comprehensiveness $(F(2, 283) = 14.52, p < .001, \eta_p2 = .09)$, and relevance $(F(2, 283) = 17.59, p < .001, \eta_p2 = .11)$. The means and standard deviations are reported in table 14.1.

All of the significant differences were either between the low likes condition and the medium likes/high likes conditions or all three conditions. When looking at the results where the low likes condition was significantly different than the medium likes/high likes conditions all of the variables were greater for the medium likes/high likes conditions with the exception of discouragement which was lower. Essentially, in the low likes condition, people felt less enjoyment, meaningfulness, and information comprehensiveness but more discouragement than those in the medium likes/high likes conditions where the attitudes plateaued.

When looking at the results where all of the conditions were significantly different the results were linear such that the low likes condition had the lowest mean, the medium likes condition had the middle mean, the high likes condition had the highest mean. For these variables, in the low likes condition, people felt less entertainment, encouragement, frequency of feedback, competence, autonomy, relatedness, and surveillance but that mean significantly increased for those in the medium likes condition then again for those in high likes condition.

Table 14.1 Summary of means and standard deviations for significant differences between dependent variables for number of incorrect answers

Dependent Variable	Low Likes	Medium Likes	High Likes
Enjoyment	3.52, 1.95[a]	5.13, 1.65[b]	5.50, 1.26[b]
Entertainment	3.56, 2.00[a]	5.17, 1.59[b]	5.65. 1.25[c]
Meaningfulness	3.34, 1.92[a]	4.43, 1.93[b]	4.87, 1.77[b]
Discouragement	3.70, 2.18[a]	2.67, 1.80[b]	2.66, 2.10[b]
Encouragement	3.00,1.96[a]	4.58, 1.83[b]	5.39, 1.36[c]
Frequency	2.93, 1.82[a]	4.26, 1.52[b]	5.07, 1.35[c]
Competence	3.84, 1.75[a]	4.87, 1.49[b]	5.46, 1.06[c]
Autonomy	4.30, 1.63[a]	4.81, 1.43[b]	5.17, 1.10[c]
Relatedness	3.63, 1.73[a]	4.87, 1.45[b]	5.40, 1.04[c]
Surveillance	2.62, 1.76[a]	3.57, 1.67[b]	4.19, 1.67[c]
Information comprehensiveness	4.26, 1.70[a]	5.01, 1.38[b]	5.22, 1.27[b]
Relevance	4.18, 1.46[a]	4.87, 1.26[b]	5.11, 1.29[b]

According to Bonferroni correction, those that do not share a superscript differ at $p < .05$ or less. If they share a superscript, they are not significantly different.

These findings are particularly interesting because of how they compare to the media feedback frequency chapter and the user media feedback and system media feedback chapter. This shows that volume of feedback is not necessarily equivalent to frequency of feedback. In addition, the context appears to be critical. Feedback from other platform users is viewed differently than feedback from other platform users on a product as seen in the user media feedback and system media feedback chapter. But broadly, this shows that the more liked content is, the more pleasant experience the user will have. On top of this, the low like condition drove a portion of the results indicating that there may be a baseline of likes that are optimum for certain variables, and once a person attains that many likes, he or she is satisfied.

In order to fully test mediation, the PROCESS macro (Hayes, 2018) was used.

Competence, autonomy, relatedness, discouragement, encouragement, frequency, surveillance, information comprehensiveness, and relevance were entered as mediators. Enjoyment was entered as the outcome variable. The volume of likes was entered as the independent variable. Age, gender, race, income, use of social media, posting on social media, liking social media, and likes on posts were entered as covariates. Model 4 using 2,000 bootstrap samples and 95 percent CI, was employed. The direct effect of the condition dissipated but there were indirect effects on enjoyment via discouragement (point estimate = .10, Boot SE = .04, CI [.04, .18]), encouragement (point estimate = .41, Boot SE = .10, CI [.22, .63]), and relatedness (point estimate = .28, Boot SE = .09, CI [.11, .45]).

The same PROCESS model was run using meaningfulness as the outcome variable. The direct effect of the condition dissipated but there were indirect effects on enjoyment via encouragement (point estimate = .55, Boot SE = .12, CI [.32, .78]), and surveillance (point estimate = .34, Boot SE = .08, CI [.20, .50]).

The same PROCESS model was run a third time using entertainment as the outcome variable. The direct effect of the condition dissipated but there were indirect effects on enjoyment via encouragement (point estimate = .34, Boot SE = .11, CI [.15, .57]), discouragement (point estimate = .08, Boot SE = .03, CI [.03, .15]), feedback frequency (point estimate = .25, Boot SE = .09, CI [.09, .42]), relatedness (point estimate = .30, Boot SE = .09, CI [.13, .50]), and information comprehensiveness (point estimate = .09, Boot SE = .04, CI [.02, .19]).

These analyses help to uncover why more likes are resulting in more enjoyment, meaningfulness, and entertainment. For enjoyment, discouragement, encouragement, and relatedness were critical. For meaningfulness, encouragement and surveillance were critical. For entertainment, discouragement, encouragement, information comprehensiveness, feedback frequency, and relatedness were critical.

Lastly, the prescribed hierarchical regression was used. In step 1, age, gender, race, income, use of social media, posting on social media, liking social media, and likes on posts were entered. In step 2, feelings of discouragement, encouragement, frequency, likelihood of purchase, competence, autonomy, relatedness, information accuracy, cognitive load, surveillance, information comprehensibility, information comprehensiveness, and information relevance were entered. In step 3, the condition was entered. Enjoyment was entered as the dependent variable. These results are detailed in table 14.2. This was run twice more with meaningfulness entered as the dependent variable and entertainment entered as the dependent variable (table 14.3 and 14.4).

Enjoyment was positively predicted by encouragement, relatedness, and information accuracy, but negatively predicted by liking social media, discouragement, and relevance. The positive predictors seem intuitive, but the negative predictors are somewhat surprising. One might expect that if someone liked social media, they would enjoy it more. Indeed, this relationship should be nearly tautological, yet it is not. Perhaps for people who do not like social media, seeing different numbers of likes was novel and therefore enjoyable but this is only conjecture. The negative relationship with relevance is similarly compelling. Typically, relevance is an important factor for media such that people are attracted to media that is of importance to them. Perhaps this was a spurious finding in this specific context as the experiment did not have the participant actually post. Or perhaps social media provides an escape and thus relevance becomes less critical.

Meaningfulness was positively predicted by feelings of encouragement and surveillance, but negatively by information comprehensibility. Again, it is puzzling that lower information quality would predict meaningfulness. Perhaps when it comes to social media likes, understanding the information is less important than being liked.

Entertainment was positively predicted by encouragement, feedback frequency, relatedness, and information accuracy. Entertainment was negatively predicted by discouragement and feelings of relevance. These results are not terribly surprising with the exception of the relevance finding. Again, this may have been spurious in the specific context but worth noting.

These findings continue to shed light on the nature of media feedback but, most importantly, this shows that volume of feedback information from other users is a noteworthy factor when examining the psychological impact of feedback.

Table 14.2 Regression Analysis for Enjoyment

	B	SE	β
Step 1			
Gender	-.28	.21	-.08
Age	.03	.01	.19[b]
Race	-.08	.06	-.07
Income	.00	.03	.01
Liking social media	.30	.10	.23[c]
Use of social media	.00	.00	-.05
Posting on social media	.00	.01	.01
Likes on posts	.00	.00	.05
	$F(8, 293) = 3.56^b$		
	Adj. R^2 = .06		
Step 2			
Gender	-.05	.13	-.01
Age	.01	.01	.05
Race	.01	.04	.01
Income	.00	.02	.00
Liking social media	-.11	.05	-.08[a]
Use of social media	.00	.00	-.03
Posting on social media	.00	.00	.00
Likes on posts	.00	.00	.00
Discouraging	-.16	.04	-.18[c]
Encouraging	.32	.05	.35[c]
Frequency	.10	.05	.10
Competence	.08	.07	.07
Autonomy	-.06	.08	-.04
Relatedness	.33	.07	.28[c]
Cognitive Load	-.11	.06	-.08
Surveillance	-.02	.05	-.02
Information Accuracy	.22	.06	.18[b]
Information Comprehensibility	.02	.08	.01
Information Comprehensiveness	.08	.07	.06
Relevance	-.18	.08	-.14[a]
	$F(11, 293) = 28.66^c$		
	Adj. R^2 = .65		
Step 3			
Gender	-.04	.13	-.01
Age	.01	.01	.01
Race	.00	.04	.00
Income	-.01	.02	-.01
Liking social media	-.12	.05	-.09[a]
Use of social media	.00	.00	-.03
Posting on social media	.00	.00	.00
Likes on posts	.00	.00	.00
Discouraging	-.15	.04	-.17[c]
Encouraging	.31	.05	.34[c]
Frequency	.09	.05	.08

(Continued)

Table 14.2   Regression Analysis for Enjoyment (*Continued*)

	B	SE	β
Competence	.06	.07	.05
Autonomy	-.04	.08	-.03
Relatedness	.32	.07	.27[c]
Cognitive Load	.12	.06	-.09
Surveillance	-.03	.05	-.03
Information Accuracy	.22	.06	.18[b]
Information Comprehensibility	.02	.08	.01
Information Comprehensiveness	.08	.07	.07
Relevance	-.19	.08	-.14[a]
Condition	.13	.10	.06

$$F(1, 293) = 27.44^c$$
$$\text{Adj. } R^2 = .65$$

[a] $p < 0.05$. [b] $p < 0.01$, [c] $p < 0.001$. No superscript $p > 0.05$.

Table 14.3 Regression Analysis for Meaningfulness

	B	SE	β
Step 1			
Gender	.10	.16	.02
Age	.00	.01	-.03
Race	.00	.05	.00
Income	-.01	.03	-.01
Liking social media	.14	.06	.10[a]
Use of social media	.00	.00	-.01
Posting on social media	.00	.01	.02
Likes on posts	.00	.00	.00
	$F_{(8, 293)} = 3.31$[b]		
	Adj. $R^2 = .06$		
Step 2			
Gender	.10	.16	.02
Age	.00	.01	-.03
Race	.00	.05	.00
Income	-.01	.03	-.01
Liking social media	.14	.06	.10[a]
Use of social media	.00	.00	-.01
Posting on social media	.00	.01	.02
Likes on posts	.00	.00	.00
Discouraging	-.05	.05	-.05
Encouraging	.42	.07	.42[c]
Frequency	-.07	.06	-.06
Competence	.11	.09	.09
Autonomy	-.09	.09	-.07
Relatedness	.10	.09	.08
Cognitive Load	-.03	.08	.02
Surveillance	.33	.07	.30[c]
Information Accuracy	.10	.08	.08
Information Comprehensibility	-.21	.10	-.13[a]
Information Comprehensiveness	.07	.09	.06
Relevance	.00	.09	.01
	$F_{(12, 293)} = 18.79$[c]		
	Adj. $R^2 = .55$		
Step 3			
Gender	.07	.16	.02
Age	.00	.01	.03
Race	.01	.05	.01
Income	.00	.03	.00
Liking social media	.12	.07	.09
Use of social media	.00	.00	-.01
Posting on social media	.00	.01	.01
Likes on posts	.00	.00	-.02
Discouraging	-.06	.05	-.06
Encouraging	.43	.07	.43[c]
Frequency	-.04	.06	-.04

(Continued)

Chapter 14

Table 14.3   Regression Analysis for Meaningfulness (*Continued*)

	B	SE	β
Competence	.14	.09	.11
Autonomy	-.12	.09	-.09
Relatedness	.12	.09	.10
Cognitive Load	-.02	.08	-.01
Surveillance	.35	.07	.32[c]
Information Accuracy	.10	.08	.07
Information Comprehensibility	-.20	.10	-.12[a]
Information Comprehensiveness	.07	.09	.05
Relevance	.01	.09	.01
Condition	-.22	.13	-.09
	$F(1, 293) = 18.18$[c]		
	Adj. $R^2 = .55$		

[a] $p < 0.05$. [b] $p < 0.01$, [c] $p < 0.001$. No superscript $p > 0.05$.

Table 14.4   Regression Analysis for Entertainment

	B	SE	β
Step 1			
Gender	-.17	.22	-.04
Age	.02	.01	.14[a]
Race`	-.07	.06	-.07
Income	-.02	.03	-.04
Liking social media	.28	.08	.21
Use of social media	.00	.00	.04
Posting on social media	.00	.01	.02
Likes on posts	.00	.00	.06
	$F(8, 293) = 2.60$[b]		
	Adj. $R^2 = .07$		
Step 2			
Gender	.10	.13	.03
Age	.00	.01	.04
Race`	.03	.04	.03
Income	-.02	.02	-.04
Liking social media	.09	.05	.06
Use of social media	.00	.00	-.03
Posting on social media	.00	.00	-.01
Likes on posts	.00	.00	-.01
Discouraging	-.13	.04	-.15[b]
Encouraging	.27	.05	.22[c]
Frequency	.22	.05	.22[c]
Competence	.10	.07	.09
Autonomy	-.05	.07	-.04
Relatedness	.35	.07	.30[c]
Cognitive Load	-.10	.06	-.08
Surveillance	.01	.05	.01
Information Accuracy	.21	.06	.17[b]
Information Comprehensibility	.20	.06	.16[b]
Information Comprehensiveness	.13	.07	.11
Relevance	-.30	.08	-.22[c]
	$F(12, 293) = 31.03$[c]		
	Adj. $R^2 = .69$		
Step 3			
Gender	.11	.13	.03
Age	.01	.01	.04
Race`	.03	.04	.02
Income	-.03	.02	-.05
Liking social media	.10	.05	.07
Use of social media	.00	.00	-.03
Posting on social media	.00	.00	.00
Likes on posts	.00	.00	.00
Discouraging	-.12	.04	-.14[b]
Encouraging	.26	.05	.28[c]
Frequency	.21	.05	.20[c]

(Continued)

Table 14.4 Regression Analysis for Entertainment (*Continued*)

	B	SE	β
Competence	.09	.07	.07
Autonomy	-.04	.08	-.03
Relatedness	.33	.07	.29c
Cognitive Load	-.12	.06	-.09
Surveillance	.00	.05	.00
Information Accuracy	.21	.06	.17b
Information Comprehensibility	-.01	.08	-.01
Information Comprehensiveness	.13	.07	.11
Relevance	-.31	.08	-.23c
Condition	.14	.10	.06
	$F(1, 293) = 29.77$c		
	Adj. $R^2 = .67$		

[a]$p < 0.05$. [b]$p < 0.01$, [c]$p < 0.001$. No superscript $p > 0.05$.

Chapter 15

Dating Apps and Feedback Loops

Online dating or the act of finding a romantic partner via the internet has become more and more common in the last several years such that it is not abnormal for people to meet one another in a mediated setting and develop a relationship. This is, of course, contrary to meeting a partner via traditional social channels such as through friends or in-person social gatherings. In this chapter, the feedback loops created in online dating are examined. This is of particular import because it shows how media feedback loops are altering traditional aspects of daily life.

One reason that online dating has become so popular and such a big business—there are a multitude of dating apps and platforms that one can choose from—this chapter argues is that dating apps provide a media feedback loop that traditional dating may not. This helps to explain the appeal and growth of online dating.

Online dating apps allow people who may not be comfortable in more traditional settings to explore dating options, especially those who are sensitive to rejection (Hance, Blackhart, & Dew, 2018). Indeed, results from this study indicated that people were more likely to be honest about who they were on online dating platforms and thus, were more likely to use the platforms. Ferrer (2019) suggested that through mediation people are empowered to legitimize their identity. By legitimizing their identity, people choose to share or keep private for a more controlled feedback loop of acceptance and rejection. In fact, features of online dating websites often attempt to minimize negative outcomes for users in order to reduce the negative outcomes of the feedback loop (Ferrer, 2019).

In one study, people either met via text-based chat or via videoconferencing technology (Antheunis, Schouten, & Walther, 2019). After this initial encounter, the pairs met face-to-face. There was more social attraction between the people who had used text-based chat instead of videoconferencing technology. This demonstrates the way in which CMC might tap into important factors of a feedback loop as well as in a relationship. Another study showed that online dating apps allowed people to gather information on possible partners, and this information gathering process allowed users to filter their preferences such that people tended to be attracted to others who were perceived to have similarities to the user such as political beliefs, educational background, and race (Huber & Malhotra, 2017).

In sum, empirical research suggests that online dating is appealing because of the affordances it allows. In other words, the feedback mechanisms implemented on online dating apps provide a desirable experience for many who would might uncomfortable dating otherwise, or for those who desire a more feedback driven dating experience.

METHOD

Please note that this chapter deviates in part from the method and measures outlined previously in this book. For this chapter, a survey was used to explore the feedback loops in dating apps. Respondents were asked to fill out a questionnaire detailing their attitudes and perceptions related to dating apps. Respondents were also asked how often they used dating apps, how many connections they have made on dating apps, and whether or not they were in a relationship as a result of using a dating app.

Measures

Participants were also asked a series of open-ended questions which included: "What are the best parts about using a dating app?" "What are the worst parts about using a dating app?" "What are the most important features and functions of a dating app?" "Why have you/do you use a dating app?" "Are you satisfied with the dating apps you have used? Why or why not?" "What dating apps have you used? Why?" and "Have you stopped using any dating apps? Why?"

These questions were selected as they would give respondents an opportunity to respond, in their own words, about their experiences. Dating apps are, ostensibly, transparent in their feedback loop goals—people connect with one another with the aim of developing some form of relationship. Thus, the goal in this case can be safely assumed and responses can be interpreted in kind.

Each of the quantitative measures used previously indicated acceptable reliability (competence $\alpha = .88$, autonomy $\alpha = .82$, relatedness $\alpha = .84$, surveillance $\alpha = .81$, cognitive load $\alpha = .80$, information comprehensiveness α

= .86). For information accuracy, the item, "The information is not precise" was removed and the remaining two items were correlated, $r = .75$ $p < .01$. For, information comprehensibility, "The information is not presented in an adequate way" was removed, $\alpha = .86$. For relevance, "the information does not help me at all" was removed, $r = .62$ $p < .01$.

Participants

After removing participants who failed the attention checks, eighty-seven remained. The participants were majority white (69.0%) males (63.2%) in their late-30s ($M = 36.82$), and 57.5 percent made $59,999 or less. The sample on average used dating apps 4.98 times a week, connected with an average of 20.23 people, and 54.7 percent were in a relationship with someone met through a dating app.

RESULTS

First, the open-ended data will be presented and discussed, second the quantitative survey results will be provided.

When asked "What are the best parts about using a dating app?" respondents tended to talk about several key themes. First was "meeting people" such that dating apps allowed users to meet one another. For example, one person said, "I like seeing who is single around me, a new way to meet people" and another said:

> The best part is that for someone like me, who had 2 jobs in which I primarily worked with women or married men, it allowed me to expand the number of people I could meet. I didn't have much opportunity to meet anyone at work, where I spent most of my time. Plus, I was a teacher, and it's not appropriate to use a school setting to meet people. So the dating apps increased my chances of meeting someone . . .

Building off of this, a sub-theme was that dating apps provided an alternative way of meeting people outside of traditional social interactions. Respondents said things like, "Being able to meet people without having to go to a club/bar" was the best part and someone else said, "I get to meet people I wouldn't normally meet."

The second theme spoke to the convenience of dating apps focusing on affordances such that they were "fast" and "easy" to use. "It is quick and easy to find a person with a personality similar to yours." "Most dating apps have filters to select your religion, drinking/smoking preference, pets, education, etc. so it is easy to filter out people you aren't attracted to." One said the best part of dating apps was "Ease and convenience of use; can meet lots of women quickly."

The third theme indicated that users had agency while using dating apps such that they had choice and were able to attain information. One said it was useful "having a larger pool to choose from." A few more examples follow. "You can know variety of people. You can choose ones you want to talk to and if they think the same, it's a match. So at least we have the same beginning feeling with each other." "You get a lot of information up front about a potential somebody, as well as a rough idea what they look like, before ever meeting them—that's very efficient." "You get to talk to different varieties of people around the world and get to know them."

When asked "What are the worst parts about using a dating app?" the comments mainly focused on the lack of quality people using these apps. Fake accounts seemed prevalent as many said things like, "You don't know if they are fake or not." Alongside this was a fear of catfishing—according to Urban Dictionary, "A fake or stolen online identity created or used for the purposes of beginning a deceptive relationship." "Sometimes you may not be talking to the same person who you think you are talking to, could be a catfish."

If there was not a fear of fake accounts, there was a fear that other users were bad actors. For example, "some people have bad intentions," "there are perverts and weird people on there sometimes," and "the worst parts are meeting freaks." Besides issues of safety, this can be viewed through another comment, that these apps are time-consuming. One said, they are a "waste of time" and another said, "You can often get a date faster in real life. The time you put into it often does not pay off." This was also mentioned in conjunction with ghosting (according to Urban Dictionary, "when a person cuts off all communication with their friends or the person they're dating, with zero warning or notice before hand") because people you are talking to "tend to ghost and waste a lot of time."

When asked about the best features of dating apps, features that allowed for information gathering and blocking were frequently mentioned. Specifically, people liked being able to see pictures of others to assess attraction, see others' locations to know if people are nearby, and look at profile information to see if others might be a match. Dovetailing with this was a desire for "filters" and ways to "block" other users.

When asked why they use dating apps the answers were nearly unanimous—to meet people. However, some people were looking for serious committed relationships, others were looking for friendships, some were looking for casual intimacy, and others were just passing the time or having fun by chatting with others.

As for satisfaction with dating apps, many were satisfied with them because they had met people, or they had achieved some physical or psychological reward. For example, some said, I "met the man I married," and another said, "I bedded plenty of women, and eventually met one I actually liked." Otherwise, these dating apps, "keep me calm" and "give relief from stress."

When people were not satisfied with dating apps it was almost exclusively because they had not met someone through the apps that was satisfactory. "I mean, I'm still single so I wouldn't say satisfied. Satisfied would be if I met someone through a dating app and was in a relationship with them." "I was unsatisfied . . . because of scammers, people looking for sex, etc." "Eh, it's been kinda lame so far. I haven't really connected with someone."

When asked, "What dating apps have you used? Why?" People stated that they used ones that have the most options, are most "widely known/highly rated," or meet specific goals. One said they used ones that "have been recommended or I saw them in news articles." By using "the popular ones at the time and had the most users, I didn't limit myself with a smaller, more obscure app." One person said that they used a specific one because it required payment "because I thought I'd have better luck and there'd be more quality control on it." Another said that one was "a high-quality application, registration is free and has a personality test, which for me is one of the main factors."

When asked "Have you stopped using any dating apps? Why?" people had either met someone or felt it was not meeting their goals. Consider the following quotes, "I use [one] more than [another] now, I am looking for a more serious relationship, not just a hook up." "I have stopped using them because I am now in a relationship." "Yes, because I wasn't getting anywhere."

These results are quite compelling when using the lens of media feedback. They show a clear pattern of a feedback loop created by dating apps. People used these apps in order to meet others—though the conditions of meeting someone may vary. People liked the apps when the apps had features that allowed for goal accomplishment. They disliked the apps when the apps or the people on the apps worked against the goals. People stopped using apps when they had met their goal of meeting someone or they felt that the app was no longer viable for achieving the stated goal. To put these findings into a tangible example, here is a hypothetical anecdote. Jason is lonely and would like to meet a partner to spend time with. He has a goal to find a partner. Jason signs up for a few dating apps, entering media feedback loops. He finds that some apps have features he likes and others that he does not. He also has progressed toward his goal with some apps and not on others. This leads him to use some apps more than others. Jason eventually meets a partner through one of his preferred dating apps and they begin a committed relationship. Jason has met his goal and thus closes his feedback loop. He exits the loop and stops using the dating apps. What was once a nearly exclusive face-to-face endeavor has been radically altered by the introduction of media feedback loops found in dating apps.

Again, the prescribed hierarchical regression was used. In step 1, age, gender, race, income, how often they used dating apps, how many people they connected with, and whether or not they were in a relationship with someone met through a dating app were entered. In step 2, feelings of discouragement, encouragement, competence, autonomy, relatedness, information accuracy, cognitive load, surveillance, information comprehensibility, information comprehensiveness, information relevance were entered. Enjoyment was entered as the dependent variable. These results are detailed in table 15.1. This was

Table 15.1   Regression Analysis for Enjoyment

	B	SE	β
Step 1			
Gender	-.38	.31	-.14
Age	.00	.01	-.08
Race	.16	.10	.18
Income	-.03	.05	-.07
Use dating app	.00	.02	-.01
People connected with	.00	.00	-.02
In relationship	-.42	.29	-.16
	$F_{(7, 84)} = 1.16$		
	Adj. $R^2 = .01$		
Step 2			
Gender	-.42	.24	-.16
Age	.00	.00	-.04
Race	.04	.08	.05
Income	-.06	.04	-.15
Use dating app	.00	.02	.00
People connected with	.00	.00	.03
In relationship	-.09	.25	-.03
Discouraging	-.09	.08	-.13
Encouraging	.25	.10	.31[a]
Frequency	.14	.13	.15
Competence	.29	.15	.23
Autonomy	.35	.16	.26[a]
Relatedness	.29	.15	.53
Cognitive Load	.15	.12	.16
Surveillance	-.01	.14	-.01
Information Accuracy	.13	.17	.15
Information Comprehensibility	-.15	.20	-.11
Information Comprehensiveness	.11	.19	.11
Relevance	.20	.16	.19
	$F_{(12, 84)} = 5.29^{c}$		
	Adj. $R^2 = .49$		

[a]$p < 0.05$. [b]$p < 0.01$, [c]$p < 0.001$. No superscript $p > 0.05$.

run twice more with meaningfulness entered as the dependent variable and entertainment entered as the dependent variable (table 15.2 and 15.3).

Enjoyment was only predicted by feelings of encouragement and autonomy. Meaningfulness was positively predicted by the number of people connected with, discouragement, relatedness, surveillance, and information comprehensiveness. Meaningfulness was negatively predicted by more frequent use of the app and information comprehensibility. Entertainment was positively predicted by feelings of discouragement, encouragement, and competence. Entertainment was negatively predicted by cognitive load and information comprehensibility.

Table 15.2   Regression Analysis for Meaningfulness

	B	*SE*	*β*
Step 1			
Gender	.10	.38	.03
Age	.00	.01	.05
Race	.38	.12	.34[b]
Income	-.02	.06	-.04
Use dating app	-.01	.02	-.06
People connected with	.00	.00	.10
In relationship-.80	.25	-.34[a]	
	$F_{(7, 84)} = 2.52$[a]		
	Adj. $R^2 = .11$		
Step 2			
Gender	.14	.21	.04
Age	.00	.00	.05
Race	.13	.07	.12
Income	-.01	.03	-.02
Use dating app	-.05	.01	-.24[b]
People connected with	.00	.01	.13[a]
In relationship	.10	.22	.03
Discouraging	.21	.07	.21[b]
Encouraging	.10	.09	.10
Frequency	.14	.12	.12
Competence	.14	.13	.09
Autonomy	-.09	.14	-.05
Relatedness	.36	.14	.42[b]
Cognitive Load	-.12	.10	-.10
Surveillance	.47	.12	.35[c]
Information Accuracy	.17	.15	.16
Information Comprehensibility	-.68	.17	-.37[c]
Information Comprehensiveness	.66	.17	.53[c]
Relevance	-.22	.14	-.16
	$F_{(12, 84)} = 14.56$[c]		
	Adj. $R^2 = .75$		

[a] $p < 0.05$. [b] $p < 0.01$, [c] $p < 0.001$. No superscript $p > 0.05$

Table 15.3   Regression Analysis for Entertainment

	B	SE	β
Step 1			
Gender	.20	.29	.08
Age	.00	.01	-.01
Race	.01	.09	-.02
Income	.05	.05	.12
Use dating app	.02	.02	.13
People connected with	.00	.00	-.09
In relationship	-,14	,27	-.06
	$F_{(7, 84)} = .34$		
	Adj. $R^2 = .06$		
Step 2			
Gender	.02	.23	.01
Age	.00	.00	.01
Race	.10	.08	.13
Income	.03	.04	.08
Use dating app	.00	.02	.00
People connected with	.00	.00	.17
In relationship	.40	.25	.17
Discouraging	.19	.07	.31[a]
Encouraging	.20	.09	.27[a]
Frequency	-.01	.13	-.01
Competence	.40	.14	.35[b]
Autonomy	.16	.15	.14
Relatedness	.21	.15	.27
Cognitive Load	-.23	.11	-.26[a]
Surveillance.20	.13	.21	
Information Accuracy	-.11	.16	-.14
Information Comprehensibility	-.29	.19	-.23[c]
Information Comprehensiveness	.09	.19	.11
Relevance.02	.16	.02	
	$F_{(12, 84)} = 4.17^c$		
	Adj. $R^2 = .42$		

[a]$p < 0.05$. [b]$p < 0.01$, [c]$p < 0.001$. No superscript $p > 0.05$.

Those looking for deeper relationships tended to find meaning when connecting to others. Those finding enjoyment and entertainment seemed to enjoy the chase with some encouragement, some discouragement, and a bit of mystery through a lack of information quality. Regardless, this chapter plainly demonstrates the way in which media feedback systems have altered a routine part of daily life.

Chapter 16

Conclusion

Takeaways and the Future of Feedback

The aim of this book was to provide clarity around the concept of media feedback and allow for a more appropriate and deeper understanding of what feedback is but also what it is not. Ultimately, readers should feel that feedback is more complex than they had, perhaps, previously thought.

In the bulk of this book, the assumed essential traits of feedback, based on previous literature, were tested and unpacked with some expected and unexpected results. Some of the assumptions about feedback might actually be contingent upon other factors that are more salient and indicate a more elaborate model than some have formerly theorized. Media feedback loops were also examined with specific attention to CMC given that many of the feedback loops encountered are on social media sites. This final chapter allows an opportunity to take a macro view of the book to provide some insight into media feedback as a whole.

Many of the assumptions about feedback and how it works are tested and consequently challenged in this book. To summarize, some of the traits that are assumed to make feedback more effective did not necessarily do so, or at least were subsumed by other traits that were more prominent. One of the items that seemed to be critical but is not built into the existing research is whether or not the feedback is important to the user. With media feedback, a content creator cannot assume that a feedback loop on its own will resonate with a user. This book lays out a clear argument for that. In the case that a media feedback loop resonates with an individual, established best practices for feedback are likely more effective. However, those best practices need to be revisited when the media feedback loop does not resonate with the user.

Fortunately, there is already a theoretical framework to build off of with the ELM. The ELM is a dual-process model that describes how a persuasive message is received (Petty & Cacioppo, 1979; Petty & Cacioppo, 1990;

Petty, Cacioppo, & Schumann, 1983). When people are invested in a topic, they pay attention to certain attributes of a message and when people are not invested in a topic, they pay attention to other attributes of a message. The same theorizing can be used for media feedback loops. When a user is invested in a media feedback loop different processes, preconditions, and factors are going to be more relevant than if a user is not invested in a media feedback loop. When the user is not invested, different processes, preconditions, and factors are going to be more relevant. Media feedback loops have either penetrated a user's interest or not and there are likely degrees of penetration that merit exploration. Content creators should be mindful of what degree of penetration their content has achieved and build their feedback loops accordingly.

Another overarching finding is that feedback is more complex than it is often treated in communication research. Again, feedback needs to be thought of as a process, not simply information. Hopefully this book has demonstrated that when feedback is treated as a process, this not only creates consistency for the concept across disciplines, but it makes the concept more applicable and more reflective of the media experiences we have. The pieces of feedback are input value, goal value, and communication regarding the discrepancy between input value and goal value. From there the loop can continue or stop.

From a methodological standpoint, the measures used for information accuracy and relevance were inadequate. In nearly every chapter, those measures failed to achieve internal consistency with the originally suggested measures. In almost every case, an item needed to be removed. Perhaps this is because these measures were not attuned to studies on media feedback or the measures need to be reevaluated. Consider this a call for better measures of relevance and information accuracy with regard to studies on media feedback.

Perhaps the most important takeaway from this book is that feelings of encouragement were significant in nearly every study. Intuitively, this makes sense. Media feedback should encourage people in order to be effective. However, up until now, there has been limited research to support this specific proposition. Regardless of the context, encouragement was an important factor. Content creators should keep this top of mind.

While not as ubiquitous as encouragement, feelings of autonomy were regularly significant in this book's studies. This is not as intuitive as encouragement but does have a strong theoretical backbone. Autonomy is one of the key dimensions of self-determination theory (Ryan & Deci, 2000). When people feel autonomy, they are more intrinsically motivated which can make the feedback more effective. Also, leaning on uses and gratifications theory, people want to arrange their media diet to fit their needs. In a media environment rife with feedback loops, users need to be empowered to choose which loops they enter and which they do not in order to feel gratified.

There were other important factors that emerged from chapter to chapter based on the study and the context of the media feedback but none as frequent as encouragement and autonomy.

If the previous pages were not enough to convince readers of the importance of media feedback, the book will close with one final pilot study. A recent trend in video games allows players to buy "season passes," "battle passes," or something with a similar name. In popular games like *Fortnite* and *Call of Duty*, players have the option to buy access to a battle pass. The battle pass provides access to in-game rewards such as new characters and character skins, weapons and weapon skins among other cosmetic rewards with an occasional boost for experience or in-game currency.

One might assume that buying the battle pass would provide all of this to the player outright but that is not the case. The player has to unlock all of these rewards by playing the game and earning experience points. As players gain experience points in these games, they rank up and one of these rewards is associated with each rank. Notably, these passes expire roughly each month. If a player has not earned rewards by the time the pass expires, then the rewards disappear, and the player has the option to buy the next month's pass. In essence, players are paying an additional fee in a game for the ability to temporarily access a feedback loop that is embedded deeper in the game. This notion that people are willing to pay for additional feedback systems that requires additional "work" from the player is a relatively new widespread phenomenon and speaks to the human desire for feedback loops.

In this final study, people who had purchased these season passes were asked to take notes on their experiences with the game after having bought the season pass. Having paid for and used a battle pass led to a few common themes.

Players felt more invested in the game. A few example quotes illustrate this point, "It was all about investment of time . . . while it could be boring, I knew I would get more XP [XP refers to experience points] . . . and that it would translate into more 'stuff.'" "I definitely felt more excited to play [after buying battle pass]." "[T]here were specific items that I sort of targeted . . . which probably increased my incentive to play." "[T]he added interest was more about just collecting things and being a completionist." "I did enjoy unlocking characters and guns . . . if I was still playing with the stock characters I'd likely give up on the Game earlier. So I'd say it was worth it." However, sometimes the lack of progress toward these rewards could be demoralizing.

Some of the players indicated that they were invested to the extent that there was a sense of identity wrapped up in the battle pass. For one player the pass allowed the player access to a character whom the player, "felt much more 'attached' to" and it made aspects of the game "familiar and comfortable." Another said, "I didn't like looking a novice" and the battle pass allowed him to look more experienced at the game.

Some even suggested that the battle pass changed the way in which they thought about and played the game. "I changed my gameplay and goals . . . my goal transitioned from 'winning' the match and taking out the competition to securing more XP." "In terms of general gameplay, the micro-missions within the game related to XP . . . [it] make[s] the game more engaging."

There were also some outright negative psychological factors that players noted. Since the battle pass was scheduled to expire there appeared to be a sense of urgency to play the game while the battle pass was active.

> I feel a need to play now because the clock is ticking on our unsecured gear. I know we have four days [until my battle pass expires], so there's a strong likelihood I will log on (even if it's for one match) to make progress toward getting more loot.

One player expressed relief when the player had earned enough battle pass rewards via in-game currency in order to buy the next month's pass.

In light of this, all of the players expressed some acknowledgement of the absurdity of what they were doing as they were toiling away, trying to earn experience for rewards that they placed no value on. "I've only used the one . . . character and painted one gun. I've earned 50+ levels in Battlepass and used 2. So it's all pointless." "I don't think I really cared about the unlockable stuff." "[T]hat crap was pointless."

In conclusion, this book has provided a large degree of information on media feedback but, if nothing else, this book serves as an invitation to more studies on an important and compelling concept. There is much room for studies expanding on the work here or deviating from it in noteworthy ways. There are also new types of media feedback emerging each day. As scholars, practitioners, and users of these media, developing an understanding of these changes and developments is incumbent upon us.

References

Adriaanse, M. A., de Ridder, Denise T. D., & de Wit, John B. F. (2009). Finding the critical cue: Implementation intentions to change one's diet work best when tailored to personally relevant reasons for unhealthy eating. *Personality and Social Psychology Bulletin, 35*(1), 60–71.

Ahn, S. J. (2011). Embodied experiences in immersive virtual environments: Effects on proenvironmental attitude and behavior (Unpublished doctoral dissertation). Stanford University, Stanford, CA.

Anand, V., Webb, A., & Wong, C. (2019, September). Mitigating the potentially demotivating effects of early and frequent feedback about goal progress. AAA.

Ansari, A., & Mela, C. F. (2003). E-customization. *Journal of Marketing Research, 40*(2), 131–145.

Antheunis, M. L., Schouten, A. P., & Walther, J. B. (2019). The hyperpersonal effect in online dating: Effects of text-based CMC vs. videoconferencing before meeting face-to-face. *Media Psychology, 23*(6), 1–20.

Ariely, D. (2000). Controlling the information flow: Effects on consumers' decision making and preferences. *Journal of Consumer Research, 27*(2), 233–248.

Ashby, W. R. (1956). *An introduction to cybernetics.* Englewood Cliffs, NJ: Prentice Hall.

Baer, R. A., Smith, G. T., & Allen, K. B. (2004). Assessment of mindfulness by self-report: The Kentucky inventory of mindfulness skills. *Assessment, 11*(3), 191–206.

Barboza, E. J. S., & da Silva, M. T. (2016, September). The importance of timely feedback to interactivity in online education. In *IFIP International Conference on Advances in Production Management Systems* (pp. 307–314). Springer, Cham.

Baumeister, R. F. (1998). The self. In D. T. Gilbert, S. T. Fiske, & G. Lindzey (Eds.), *Handbook of social psychology* (4th ed., pp. 680–740). New York: McGraw-Hill.

Bayerlein, L. (2014). Students' feedback preferences: How do students react to timely and automatically generated assessment feedback? *Assessment & Evaluation in Higher Education, 39*(8), 916–931.

Bergkvist, L., & Rossiter, J. R. (2007). The predictive validity of multiple-item versus single-item measures of the same constructs. *Journal of Marketing Research, 44*(2), 175–184.

Bernstein, J. L., & Allen, B. T. (2013). Overcoming methods anxiety: Qualitative first, quantitative next, frequent feedback along the way. *Journal of Political Science Education, 9*(1), 1–15.

Boot, W. R., Kramer, A. F., Simons, D. J., Fabiani, M., & Gratton, G. (2008). The effects of video game playing on attention, memory, and executive control. *Acta Psychologica, 129*(3), 387–398.

Bowlby, J. (1982). Attachment and loss: Retrospect and prospect. *American Journal of Orthopsychiatry, 54*(2), 664–678.

Bowman, R. F. (1982). A Pac-Man theory of motivation. Tactical implications for classroom instruction. *Educational Technology, 22*(9), 14–17.

Brasel, S., & Gips, J. (2011). Media multitasking behavior: Concurrent television and computer usage. *Cyberpsychology, Behavior & Social Networking, 14*(9), 527–534.

Briñol, P., & Petty, R. E. (2006). Fundamental processes leading to attitude change: Implications for cancer prevention communications. *Journal of Communication, 56*, S81–S104.

Brooks, S. (2015). Does personal social media usage affect efficiency and well-being? *Computers in Human Behavior, 46*, 26–23.

Brown, K. A., Billings, A. C., Murphy, B., & Puesan, L. (2018). Intersections of fandom in the age of interactive media: Esports fandom as a predictor of traditional sport fandom. *Communication & Sport, 6*(4), 418–435.

Bucy, E. (2004). Interactivity in society: Locating an elusive concept. *Information Society, 20*(5), 373–383.

Buhrmester, M., Kwang, T., & Gosling, S. D. (2011). Amazon's Mechanical Turk: A new source of inexpensive, yet high-quality data? *Perspectives on Psychological Science, 6*, 3–5. http://dx.doi.org/10.1177/ 1745691610393980

Burrow, A. L., & Rainone, N. (2017). How many likes did I get?: Purpose moderates links between positive social media feedback and self-esteem. *Journal of Experimental Social Psychology, 69*, 232–236.

Butkowski, C. P., Dixon, T. L., Weeks, K. R., & Smith, M. A. (2019). Quantifying the feminine self(ie): Gender display and social media feedback in young women's Instagram selfies. *New Media & Society, 1461444819871669, 22*(5):817–837.

Butler, D. L., & Winne, P. H. (1995). Feedback and self-regulated learning: A theoretical synthesis. *Review of Educational Research, 65*(3), 245–281.

Campbell, M. C., & Kirmani, A. (2000). Consumers' use of persuasion knowledge: The effects of accessibility and cognitive capacity on perceptions of an influence agent. *Journal of Consumer Research, 27*(1), 69–83.

Card, S., Robertson, G., & Mackinlay, J. (1991). The information visualizer, an information workspace. Paper presented at the ACM Computer Human Interaction (CHI) Conference.

Carnagey, N. L., & Anderson, C. A. (2005). The effects of reward and punishment in violent video games on aggressive affect, cognition, and behavior. *Psychological Science, 16*(11), 882–889.

Carver, C., & Scheier, M. (2001). *On the self-regulation of behavior.* Cambridge, UK: Cambridge University Press.

Celis-Morales, C., Livingstone, K. M., Petermann-Rocha, F., Navas-Carretero, S., San-Cristobal, R., O'Donovan, C. B., ... & Daniel, H. (2019). Frequent nutritional feedback, personalized advice, and behavioral changes: Findings from the European Food4Me Internet-based RCT. *American Journal of Preventive Medicine, 57*(2), 209–219.

Celsi, R. L., & Olson, J. C. (1988). The role of involvement in attention and comprehension processes. *Journal of Consumer Research, 15*(2), 210–224.

Connellan, T., & Zemke, R. (1993). *Sustaining knock your socks off service.* New York, NY: AMACOM Books.

Costa, J., Adams, A. T., Jung, M. F., Guimbretière, F., & Choudhury, T. (2016, September). EmotionCheck: Leveraging bodily signals and false feedback to regulate our emotions. In *Proceedings of the 2016 ACM International Joint Conference on Pervasive and Ubiquitous Computing* (pp. 758–769).

Cronshaw, S. F., & Lord, R. G. (1987). Effects of categorization, attribution, and encoding processes on leadership perceptions. *Journal of Applied Psychology, 72*(1), 97.

Crystal, A., & Kalyanaraman, S. (2004). Usability, cognition, and affect in web interfaces: The role of informative feedback and descriptive labeling. Paper presented at the International Communication Association.

Csikszentmihalyi, M. (1990). *Flow: The psychology of optimal experience.* New York, NY: Harper Collins.

Davis, F. D., Bagozzi, R. P., & Warshaw, P. R. (1992). Extrinsic and intrinsic motivation to use computers in the workplace 1. *Journal of Applied Social Psychology, 22*(14), 1111–1132.

Deng, Q., Franke, M., Hribernik, K., & Thoben, K. D. (2017). Exploring the integration of social media feedback for user-oriented product development. In *DS 87-4 Proceedings of the 21st International Conference on Engineering Design (ICED 17) Vol 4: Design Methods and Tools, Vancouver, Canada, 21-25.08. 2017* (pp. 453–462).

DiClemente, C. C., Marinilli, A. S., Singh, M., & Bellino, L. E. (2001). The role of feedback in the process of health behavior change. *American Journal of Health Behavior, 25*(3), 217–227.

Drolet, A., & Luce, M. (2004). The rationalizing effects of cognitive load on emotion-based trade-off avoidance. *Journal of Consumer Research, 31*(1), 63–77.

Dunham, P., & Mueller, R. (1993). Effect of fading knowledge of results on acquisition, retention, and transfer of a simple motor skill. *Percept. Mot. Skills, 77,* 1187–1192.

Emmons, K. M., Wong, M., Puleo, E., Weinstein, N., Fletcher, R., & Colditz, G. (2004). Tailored computer-based cancer risk communication: Correcting colorectal cancer risk perception. *Journal of Health Communication: International Perspectives, 9*(2), 127–141.

Eom, S. B., Wen, H. J., & Ashill, N. (2006). The determinants of students' perceived learning outcomes and satisfaction in university online education: An empirical investigation. *Decision Sciences Journal of Innovative Education, 4*(2), 215–235.

Ferrer, M. M. (2019). Love interfaces: Identity and attachment in online dating. *Journal of Catalan Studies (JOCS), 1*(21), 45–53.

Finley, K. (2017). Internet democracy is great … in theory. Just ask the FCC. *Wired .com*. Retrieved from https://www.wired.com/2017/05/internet-democracy-great-theory-just-ask-fcc/

Fishbach, A., & Dhar, R. (2005). Goals as excuses or guides: The liberating effect of perceived goal progress on choice. *Journal of Consumer Research, 32*(3), 370–377.

Fleming, M., & Levie, W. H. (1993). *Instructional message design: Principles from the behavioral and cognitive sciences*. Englewood Cliffs, NJ: Educational Technology Publications.

Fong, C. J., Williams, K. M., Williamson, Z. H., Lin, S., Kim, Y. W., & Schallert, D. L. (2018). "Inside out": Appraisals for achievement emotions from constructive, positive, and negative feedback on writing. *Motivation and Emotion, 42*(2), 236–257.

Fowler, G. A. (2020). Wearable tech can spot coronavirus symptoms before you even realize you're sick. *WashingtonPost.com*. Retrieved from https://www.washington-post.com/technology/2020/05/28/wearable-coronavirus-detect/

Gee, J. P. (2005). Learning by design: Good video games as learning machines. *E-Learning, 2*(1), 5–16.

Glanz, K., Schoenfeld, E. R., & Steffen, A. (2010). A randomized trial of tailored skin cancer prevention messages for adults: Project SCAPE skin cancer awareness, prevention and education. *American Journal of Public Health, 100*(4), 735–741.

Goetz, T. (2011). Harnessing the power of feedback loops. *Wired*. Retrieved from http://www.wired.com/magazine/2011/06/ff_feedbackloop/

Hance, M. A., Blackhart, G., & Dew, M. (2018). Free to be me: The relationship between the true self, rejection sensitivity, and use of online dating sites. *The Journal of Social Psychology, 158*(4), 421–429.

Hart, S. G., & Staveland, L. E. (1988). Development of NASA-TLX (Task Load Index): Results of empirical and theoretical research. In *Advances in Psychology* (Vol. 52, pp. 139–183). North-Holland.

Harter, S. (1981). A new self-report scale of intrinsic versus extrinsic orientation in the classroom: Motivational and informational components. *Developmental Psychology, 17*(3), 300–312.

Hattie, J., & Timperley, H. (2007). The power of feedback. *Review of Educational Research, 77*(1), 81–112.

Haug, S., Meyer, C., Ulbricht, S., Gross, B., Rumpf, H., & John, U. (2010). Need for cognition as a predictor and a moderator of outcome in a tailored letters smoking cessation intervention. *Health Psychology, 29*(4), 367–373.

Hawkins, R. P., Kreuter, M., Resnicow, K., Fishbein, M., & Dijkstra, A. (2008). Understanding tailoring in communicating about health. *Health Education Research, 23*(3), 454–466.

Hawkins, E. J., Lambert, M. J., Vermeersch, D. A., Slade, K. L., & Tuttle, K. C. (2004). The therapeutic effects of providing patient progress information to therapists and patients. *Psychotherapy Research, 14*(3), 308–327.

Hayes, A. F. (2012). PROCESS: A versatile computational tool for observed variable mediation, moderation, and conditional process modeling. Retrieved from http://www.afhayes.com/public/process2012.pdf

Hayes, A. (2018). *Introduction to mediation, moderation, and conditional process analysis: A regression-based approach.* New York, NY: The Guilford Press.

Heinen, L., Heuser, T., Steinschulte, A., & Walther, A. (2017). Antagonistic enzymes in a biocatalytic pH feedback system program autonomous DNA hydrogel life cycles. *Nano Letters, 17*(8), 4989–4995.

Higgins, R., Hartley, P., & Skelton, A. (2002). The conscientious consumer: Reconsidering the role of assessment feedback in student learning. *Studies in Higher Education, 27*(1), 53–64.

Hinkin, T. R., & Schriesheim, C. A. (1989). Development and application of new scales to measure the French and Raven (1959) bases of social power. *Journal of Applied Psychology, 74*(4), 561.

Hu, G. (2019). Culture and peer feedback. In K. Hyland & F. Hyland (Eds.), *Feedback in second language writing: Contexts and issues* (pp. 45–63). Cambridge University Press.

Hu, Y., Koren, Y., & Volinsky, C. (2008, December). Collaborative filtering for implicit feedback datasets. In *2008 Eighth IEEE International Conference on Data Mining* (pp. 263–272). IEEE.

Huang, S., & Zhang, Y. (2011). Motivational consequences of perceived velocity in consumer goal pursuit. *Journal of Marketing Research, 48*(6), 1045–1056.

Huber, G. A., & Malhotra, N. (2017). Political homophily in social relationships: Evidence from online dating behavior. *The Journal of Politics, 79*(1), 269–283.

Jensen, J. F. (1998). Interactivity: Tracking a new concept in media and communication studies. *Nordicom Review, 19*, 185–204.

Joachims, T., Granka, L., Pan, B., Hembrooke, H., & Gay, G. (2017, August). Accurately interpreting clickthrough data as implicit feedback. In *ACM SIGIR Forum* (Vol. 51, No. 1, pp. 4–11). New York, NY: ACM.

Jones, E., & Sigall, H. (1971). The bogus pipeline: A new paradigm for measuring affect and attitude. *Psychological Bulletin, 76*(5), 349–364.

Juul, J. (2010). *A casual revolution: Reinventing video games and their players.* Cambridge, MA. The MIT Press.

Kalyanaraman, S., & Sundar, S. (2006). The psychological appeal of personalized content in web portals: Does customization affect attitudes and behavior? *Journal of Communication, 56*(1), 110–132.

Kalyanaraman, S., & Sundar, S. S. (2008). Impression formation effects in online mediated communication. In E. Konijn, S. Utz, M. Tanis, & S. Barnes (Eds.), *Mediated interpersonal communication* (pp. 217–233). New York, NY: Routledge.

Kamali, N., & Loker, S. (2002). Mass customization: On-line consumer involvement in product design. *Journal of Computer-Mediated Communication, 7*(4).

Keefe, P. (2019). Compulsively check your smartphone? Knowing why can help you stop. *Healthline.com.* Retrieved from https://www.healthline.com/health-news/compulsive-about-checking-your-smartphone-heres-how-to-kick-the-habit

Kluger, A. N., & DeNisi, A. (1996). The effects of feedback interventions on performance: A historical review, a meta-analysis and a preliminary feedback intervention theory. *Psychological Bulletin, 119*, 254–284.

Knobloch-Westerwick, S., Sharma, N., Hansen, D. L., & Alter, S. (2005). Impact of popularity indications on readers' selective exposure to online news. *Journal of Broadcasting & Electronic Media, 49*(3), 296–313.

Lamble D., Kauranen, T., Laakso, M., & Summala, H. (1999). Cognitive load and detection thresholds in car following situations: Safety implications for using mobile (cellular) telephones while driving. *Accident Analysis and Prevention, 31*, 617–623.

Latimer, A. E., Katulak, N. A., Mowad, L., & Salovey, P. (2005). Motivating cancer prevention and early detection behaviors using psychologically tailored messages. *Journal of Health Communication, 10*, 137–155.

Lee, D., & Schoenstedt, L. J. (2011). Comparison of esports and traditional sports consumption motives. *Journal of Research, 6*, 39–44.

Lewis, B., & Linder, D. (1997). Thinking about choking? Attentional processes and paradoxical performance. *Personality and Psychology Bulletin, 23*, 937–944.

Lim, J., Zhan, A., Ko, J., Terzis, A., Szanton, S., & Gitlin, L. (2012). A closed-loop approach for improving the wellness of low-income elders at home using game consoles. *IEEE Communications Magazine, 50*(1), 44–51.

Lin, H. F. (2007). Effects of extrinsic and intrinsic motivation on employee knowledge sharing intentions. *Journal of Information Science, 33*(2), 135–149.

Lustria, M. L., Cortese, J., Noar, S. M., & Glueckauf, R. L. (2009). Computer-tailored health interventions delivered over the web: Review and analysis of key components. *Patient Education & Counseling, 74*(2), 156–173.

MacKenzie, K. (1974). Some thoughts on tutoring by written correspondence in the Open University. *Teaching at a Distance, 1*, 45–51.

Malone, T. W. (1981). Toward a theory of intrinsically motivating instruction. *Cognitive Science, 4*, 333–369.

MarketWatch. (2020). Telehealth market: Analysis and in-depth study on size trends, emerging growth factors and regional forecast to 2026. *Marketwatch .com*. Retrieved from https://www.marketwatch.com/press-release/telehealth -market-analysis-and-in-depth-study-on-size-trends-emerging-growth-factors-and -regional-forecast-to-2026-2020-05-31

Mayer, R. E., & Moreno, R. (2003). Nine ways to reduce cognitive load in multimedia learning. *Educational Psychologist, 38*(1), 43–52.

Miller, G. A., Galanter, E., & Pribram, K. H. (1960). *Plans and the structure of behavior*. New York, NY: Henry Holt and Co.

Mindell, D. (2003). *Between human and machine: Feedback, control, and computing before cybernetics*. Baltimore, MD: Johns Hopkins University Press.

Muylle, S., Moenaert, R., & Despontin, M. (2004). The conceptualization and empirical validation of web site user satisfaction. *Information & Management, 41*(5), 543–560.

Myers, B. A. (1985). The importance of percent-done progress indicators for computer human interfaces. Paper presented at ACM CHI'85 Conference.

Nabi, R. L., Walter, N., Oshidary, N., Endacott, C. G., Love-Nichols, J., Lew, Z. J., & Aune, A. (2019). Can emotions capture the elusive gain-loss framing effect? A meta-analysis. *Communication Research*, 0093650219861256.

Nelson, T. E., Clawson, R. A., & Oxley, Z. M. (1997). Media framing of a civil liberties conflict and its effect on tolerance. *American Political Science Review, 91*(3), 567–583.

Nicholson, D. E., and Schmidt, R. A. (1991). Scheduling information feedback to enhance training effectiveness. In *Proceedings of the Human Factors Society 35th Annual Meeting*. Santa Monica, CA: Human Factors Society.

Nicol, D. (2010). From monologue to dialogue: Improving written feedback processes in mass higher education. *Assessment & Evaluation in Higher Education, 35*(5), 501–517.

Nielsen, J. (1998). Response times: The three important limits. Retrieved from http://www.useit.com/papers/responsetime.html

Nielsen, J. (2003). Usability 101: Introduction to usability. *Jakob Nielsen's Alertbox*. Retrieved from www.useit.com/alertbox/20030825.html

Noar, S. M., Benac, C. N., & Harris, M. S. (2007). Does tailoring matter? Meta-analytic review of tailored print health behavior change interventions. *Psychological Bulletin, 133*(4), 673–693.

O'Keefe, D. J., & Jensen, J. D. (2006). The advantages of compliance or the disadvantages of noncompliance? A meta-analytic review of the relative persuasive effectiveness of gainframed and loss-framed messages. *Annals of the International Communication Association, 30*, 1–43. doi:10.1080/23808985.2006.11679054

O'Keefe, D. J., & Jensen, J. D. (2007). The relative persuasiveness of gainframed loss-framed messages for encouraging disease prevention behaviors: A meta-analytic review. *Journal of Health Communication, 12*, 623–644. doi:10.1080/10810730701615198

Oard, D. W., & Kim, J. (1998, July). Implicit feedback for recommender systems. In *Proceedings of the AAAI Workshop on Recommender Systems* (Vol. 83). WoUongong.

Oliver, M. B. (2008). Tender affective states as predictors of entertainment preference. *Journal of Communication, 58*, 40–61. http://dx.doi.org/10.1111/j.1460-2466.2007.00373.x

Oliver, M. B., & Bartsch, A. (2010). Appreciation as audience response: Exploring entertainment gratifications beyond hedonism. *Human Communication Research, 36*(1), 53–81. doi: 10.1111/j.1468-2958.1993.tb00304.x

Oliver, M., Bowman, N., Woolley, J., Rogers, R., Sherrick, B. & Chung, M. Y. (2016). Video games as meaningful entertainment experiences. *Psychology of Popular Media Culture, 5*(4), 390.

Oliver, M. B., & Raney, A. A. (2011). Entertainment as pleasurable and meaningful: Identifying hedonic and eudaimonic motivations for entertainment consumption. *Journal of Communication, 61*, 984–1004. doi: 10.1111/j.1460-2466.2011.01585.x

Ozbay, H. (2019). *Introduction to feedback control theory*. Routledge.

Park, E., McDaniel, A., & Jung, M. S. (2009). Computerized tailoring of health information. *CIN: Computers, Informatics, Nursing, 27*(1), 34–43.

Pekrun, R., Cusack, A., Murayama, K., Elliot, A. J., & Thomas, K. (2014). The power of anticipated feedback: Effects on students' achievement goals and achievement emotions. *Learning and Instruction, 29,* 115–124.

Pelletier, L. G., & Sharp, E. (2008). Persuasive communication and proenvironmental behaviours: How message tailoring and message framing can improve the integration of behaviours through self-determined motivation. *Canadian Psychology/ Psychologie Canadienne, 49*(3), 210–217.

Petty, R. E., & Cacioppo , J. T. (1979). Issue involvement can increase or decrease persuasion by enhancing message-relevant cognitive responses. *Journal of Personality & Social Psychology, 37*(10), 1915.

Petty, R. E., & Cacioppo, J. T. (1990). Involvement and persuasion: Tradition versus integration. *Psychological Bulletin, 107*(3), 367–374.

Petty, R. E., Cacioppo, J. T., & Schumann, D. (1983) Central and peripheral routes to advertising effectiveness: The moderating role of involvement. *Journal of Consumer Research, 10*(2), 135–146.

Poulos, A., & Mahony, M. J. (2008). Effectiveness of feedback: The students' perspective. *Assessment & Evaluation in Higher Education, 33*(2), 143–154.

Prensky, M. (2001). *Digital game-based learning.* New York: McGraw Hill.

Ramaprasad, A. (1983). On the definition of feedback. *Behavioral Science, 28*(1), 4–13.

Ramsay, J., Barbesi, A., & Preece, J. (1998). A psychological investigation of long retrieval times on the World Wide Web. *Interacting With Computers, 10*(1), 77–86.

Reeves, B., & Read, J. L. (2013). *Total engagement: How games and virtual worlds are changing the way people work and businesses compete.* Harvard Business Press.

Reinecke, L., Tamborini, R., Grizzard, M., Lewis, R., Eden, A., & Bowman, N. (2012). Characterizing mood management as need satisfaction: The effects of intrinsic needs on selective exposure and mood repair. *Journal of Communication, 62*(3), 437–453.

Rendle, S., Freudenthaler, C., Gantner, Z., & Schmidt-Thieme, L. (2012). BPR: Bayesian personalized ranking from implicit feedback. arXiv preprint arXiv:1205.2618.

Riggio, R. E., Chaleff, I., & Lipman-Blumen, J. (Eds.). (2008). *The art of followership: How great followers create great leaders and organizations* (Vol. 146). John Wiley & Sons.

Rimer, B. K., & Kreuter, M. W. (2006). Advancing tailored health communication: A persuasion and message effects perspective. *Journal of Communication, 56,* S184–S201.

Rogers, R. (2020). Boys in the booth: The impact of announcer gender on audience demand. *Journal of Sports Economics,* Vol. ahead-of-print No. ahead-of print.

Rogers, R. (2018). How sports entertain: Enjoyable and meaningful experiences for sports audiences. *Media Watch, 9*(3), 372–382.

Rogers, R. (2016). *How video games impact players: The pitfalls and benefits of a gaming society.* Lanham, MD: Lexington Books.

Rogers, R., Dillman-Carpentier, F., & Barnard, L. (2016). Media enjoyment as a function of control over characters. *Entertainment Computing, 12,* 29–39.

Rogers, R., Ivory, J., Ivory, A., Keene, J., & Cipollene, M. (n.d.). Concerning interactivity: Effective videogame content analysis. Unpublished manuscript.

Rogers, R., Woolley, J., Sherrick, B., Bowman, N, & Oliver, M. (2017). Fun versus meaningful video game experiences: A qualitative analysis of user responses. *The Computer Games Journal, 6*(1–2), 63–79.

Rosenberg, M. (1965). *Society and the adolescent self-image.* Princeton, NJ: Princeton University Press.

Rothman, A. J., & Salovey, P. (1997). Shaping perceptions to motivate healthy behavior: The role of message framing. *Psychological Bulletin, 121,* 3–19. doi:10.1037/0033-2909.121.1.3

Ruggiero, T. E. (2000). Uses and gratifications theory in the 21st century. *Mass Communication & Society, 3*(1), 3–37.

Ruiter, R., Werrij, M. Q., & de Vries, H. (2010). Investigating message-framing effects in the context of a tailored intervention promoting physical activity. *Health Education Research, 25*(2), 343–354.

Ryan, R. M., & Deci, E. L. (2000). The darker and brighter sides of human existence: Basic psychological needs as a unifying concept. *Psychological Inquiry, 11*(4), 319e338. http://dx.doi.org/10.1207/s15327965pli1104_03.

Ryan, R., Rigby, C., & Przybylski, A. (2006). The motivational pull of video games: A self-determination theory approach. *Motivation & Emotion, 30*(4), 344–360.

Sabik, N. J., Falat, J., & Magagnos, J. (2019). When self-worth depends on social media feedback: Associations with psychological well-being. *Sex Roles, 82*(2), 1–11.

Schmidt, R. A. (1991). Frequent augmented feedback can degrade learning: Evidence and interpretations. In Requin J., Stelmach G.E. (eds), *Tutorials in motor neuroscience* (pp. 59–75). Dordrecht: Springer.

Schunk, D. H. (1990). Goal setting and self-efficacy during self-regulated learning. *Educational Psychologist, 25*(1), 71.

Schunk, D. H. (1991). Self-efficacy and academic motivation. *Educational Psychologist, 26*(3/4), 207.

Schunk, D. H. (1995). Self-efficacy and education and instruction. In J. E. Maddux (Ed.), *Self-efficacy, adaptation, and adjustment: Theory, research, and application* (pp. 281–303). New York, NY: Plenum Press.

Schunk, D. H., & Pajares, F. (2002). The development of academic self-efficacy. In A. Wigfield & J. S. Eccles (Eds.), *Development of achievement motivation* (pp. 15–31). San Diego, CA: Academic Press.

Schunk, D. H., & Swartz, C. W. (1993). Goals and progress feedback: Effects on self-efficacy and writing achievement. *Contemporary Educational Psychology, 18*(3), 337–354.

Senge, P. M. (1990). *The fifth discipline.* New York, NY: Doubleday.

Sheehan, K. B. (2018). Crowdsourcing research: Data collection with Amazon's Mechanical Turk. *Communication Monographs, 85*(1), 140–156.

Shiv, B., & Huber, J. (2000). The impact of anticipating satisfaction on consumer choice. *Journal of Consumer Research, 27*(2), 202–216.

Simonson, I. (2005). Determinants of customers' responses to customized offers: Conceptual framework and research propositions. *Journal of Marketing, 69*(1), 32–45.

Smith, B. W., Dalen, J., Wiggins, K., Tooley, E., Christopher, P., & Bernard, J. (2008). The brief resilience scale: Assessing the ability to bounce back. *International Journal of Behavioral Medicine, 15*(3), 194–200.

Soman, D., & Shi, M. (2003). Virtual progress: The effect of path characteristics on perceptions of progress and choice. *Management Science, 49*, 1229–1250.

Sparrow, W. A. (1995). Acquisition and retention effects of reduced relative frequency of knowledge of results. *Australian Journal of Psychology*, 47, 97–104.

Sparrow, W. A., & Summers, J. J. (1992). Performance on trials without knowledge of results (KR) in reduced relative frequency presentations of KR. *Journal of Motor Behavior, 24*, 197–209.

Spotify.com. (2020). Made for you. *Spotify.com*. Retrieved from https://support.spotify.com/us/article/made-for-you-playlists/

Stevenson, M., & Phakiti, A. (2019). Automated feedback and second language writing. In K. Hyland & F. Hyland (Eds.), *Feedback in second language writing: Contexts and issues* (pp. 125–142). Cambridge University Press.

Sundar, S. S. (2008). *The MAIN model: A heuristic approach to understanding technology effects on credibility* (pp. 73–100). MacArthur Foundation Digital Media and Learning Initiative.

Sundar, S., Kalyanaraman, S., & Brown, J. (2003). Explicating web site interactively: Impression formation effects in political campaign sites. *Communication Research, 30*(1), 30–59.

Sundar, S. S., & Marathe, S. S. (2010). Personalization versus customization: The importance of agency, privacy, and power usage. *Human Communication Research, 36*(3), 298–322.

Sundar, S. S., & Nass, C. (2001). Conceptualizing sources in online news. *Journal of Communication, 51*(1), 52–72.

Sundar, S. S., Oeldorf-Hirsch, A., & Xu, Q. (2008). The bandwagon effect of collaborative filtering technology. In *CHI'08 extended abstracts on Human factors in computing systems* (pp. 3453–3458). Florence Italy

Sweller, J. (1988). Cognitive load during problem solving: Effects on learning. *Cognitive Science, 12*(2), 257–285.

Tamborini, R., Bowman, N. D., Eden, A. L., & Grizzard, M. (2010). Defining media enjoyment as the satisfaction of intrinsic needs. *Journal of Communication, 60*, 758–777.

Thiemann, K. S., & Goldstein, H. (2001). Social stories, written text cues, and video feedback: Effects on social communication of children with autism. *Journal of Applied Behavior Analysis, 34*(4), 425–446.

Tseng, S. T., Levy, P. E., Young, S. H. A., Thibodeau, R. K., & Zhang, X. (2019). Frequent feedback in modern organizations: Panacea or fad? In *Feedback at work* (pp. 53–73). Springer, Cham.

Valenzuela, A., & Dhar, R. (2004). Effects of preference elicitation task on consumer reactions to product customization. Paper presented at Association for Consumer Research.

Valins, S. (1966). Cognitive effects of false heart-rate feedback. *Journal of Personality and Social Psychology, 4*(4), 400.

Valkenburg, P. M., Peter, J., & Schouten, A. (2006). Friend networking sites and their relationship to adolescents' well-being and social self-esteem. *Cyberpsychology & Behavior, 9*(5), 584–590.

Värlander, S. (2008). The role of students' emotions in formal feedback situations. *Teaching in Higher Education, 13*(2), 145–156.

Veksler, A. E., & Boren, J. P. (2017). Communicatively restricted organizational stress (CROS) II: Development and validation of the CROS-14. *Communication Methods and Measures, 11*(2), 137–149.

Vrasidas, C., & McIsaac, M. S. (1999). Factors influencing interaction in an online course. *American Journal of Distance Education, 13*(3), 22–36.

Wan, H. (2008). Resonance as a mediating factor accounting for the message effect in tailored communication—Examining crisis communication in a tourism context. *Journal of Communication, 58*(3), 472–489.

Wang, H. C., Katzschmann, R. K., Teng, S., Araki, B., Giarré, L., & Rus, D. (2017, May). Enabling independent navigation for visually impaired people through a wearable vision-based feedback system. In *2017 IEEE international conference on robotics and automation (ICRA)* (pp. 6533–6540). IEEE.

Wanous, J. P., Reichers, A. E., & Hudy, M. J. (1997). Overall job satisfaction: How good are single-item measures? *Journal of Applied Psychology, 82*(2):247–52

Ward, A., & Mann, T. (2000). Don't mind if I do: Disinhibited eating under cognitive load. *Journal of Personality and Social Psychology, 78*(4), 753–763.

Webb, M. S., Simmons, V. N., & Brandon, T. H. (2005). Tailored interventions for motivating smoking cessation: Using placebo tailoring to examine the influence of expectancies and personalization. *Health Psychology, 24*, 179–188.

Weeks, D. L., & Kordus, R. N. (1998). Relative frequency of knowledge of performance and motor skill learning. *Research Quarterly for Exercise and Sport, 69*, 224–230.

Westervelt, E. R., Grizzle, J. W., Chevallereau, C., Choi, J. H., & Morris, B. (2018). *Feedback control of dynamic bipedal robot locomotion.* CRC Press.

Wheeler, S. C., DeMarree, K. G., & Petty, R. E. (2008). A match made in the laboratory: Persuasion and matches to primed traits and stereotypes. *Journal of Experimental Social Psychology, 44*(4), 1035–1047.

Wheeler, S. C., Petty, R. E., & Bizer, G. Y. (2005). Self-schema matching and attitude change: Situational and dispositional determinants of message elaboration. *Journal of Consumer Research, 31*(4), 787–797.

Wiener, N. (1961). *Cybernetics: Or, control and communication in the animal and the machine.* Cambridge, MA: MIT Press.

Williams-Piehota, P., Latimer, A. E., Katulak, N. A., Cox, A., Silvera, S. A. N., Mowad, L., & Salovey, P. (2009). Tailoring messages to individual differences in monitoring-blunting styles to increase fruit and vegetable intake. *Journal of Nutrition Education and Behavior, 41*(6), 398–405.

Winne, P. H., & Butler, D. L. (1994). Student cognition in learning from teaching. In T. Husen & T. Postlethwaite (Eds.), *International encyclopedia of education* (2nd ed., pp. 5738–5745). Oxford: Pergamon.

Winstein, C. J., & Schmidt, R. A. (1990). Reduced frequency of knowledge of results enhances motor skill learning. *Journal of Experimental Psychology: Learning, Memory, and Cognition, 16*, 677–691.

Wishart, L. R., & Lee, T. D. (1997). Effect of aging and reduced relative frequency of knowledge of results on learning of a motor skill. *Perceptual and Motor Skills, 84*, 1107–1150.

Wood, R. T. A., Griffiths, M. D., Chappell, D., & Davies, M. N. O. (2004). The structural characteristics of video games: A psycho-structural analysis. *Cyberpsychology & Behavior, 7*(1), 1–10.

Wulf, G., Chiviacowsky, S., Schiller, E., & Ávila, L. T. G. (2010). Frequent external focus feedback enhances motor learning. *Frontiers in Psychology, 1*, 190.

Wulf, G., & Schmidt, R. A. (1989). The learning of generalized motor programs: Reducing the relative frequency of knowledge of results enhances memory. *Journal of Experimental Psychology: Learning, Memory, and Cognition, 15*, 748–757.

Wulf, G., Shea, C. H., & Matschiner, S. (1998). Frequent feedback enhances complex motor skill learning. *Journal of Motor Behavior, 30*(2), 180–192.

Zamir, A. R., Wu, T. L., Sun, L., Shen, W. B., Shi, B. E., Malik, J., & Savarese, S. (2017). Feedback networks. In *Proceedings of the IEEE Conference on Computer Vision and Pattern Recognition* (pp. 1308–1317). Honolulu, Hawaii.

Zhang, Y., & Huang, S. (2010). How endowed versus earned progress affects consumer goal commitment and motivation. *Journal of Consumer Research, 37*(4), 641–654.

Index

accuracy: approach/avoid *versus* feedback, 29; information, 20, 40, 41, 124, 128, 156

acquisition, of information, 20

advertisements, user perception of, 118

agency, in dating apps, 150

Allen, K. B., 103

Amazon, 16, 126–28; Mechanical Turk, 15, 20–21, 90

analysis: for approach/avoid, 29; of content, 3; for customization in feedback, 113, 114; for distractions in feedback, 102–3, 104–6; for feedback as authority, 91; for feedback from users, 137; for frequency of feedback, 62; for implicit/explicit feedback, 50; for positive/negative feedback, 38, 41; for relevance of feedback, 81; for system generated/user generated feedback, 127; for timeliness of feedback, 72, 76; for veracity of feedback, 119, 120. *See also* results; *specific types of studies*

Analysis of Covariance (ANCOVA), 105, 114

Analysis of Variance (ANOVA): for approach/avoid, 27; for customization in feedback, 113; for distractions in feedback, 104, 105; for feedback as authority, 91; for feedback from users, 137; for positive negative feedback, 38; for relevance of feedback, 81; for system generated/user generated feedback, 127; for timeliness of feedback, 72; for veracity of feedback, 119

ANCOVA. *See* Analysis of Covariance

Anderson, C. A., 14

ANOVA. *See* Analysis of Variance

answers, incorrect: cognitive load of, *39*, 39–40; difference between dependent variables for, 117–38, *138*

approach/avoid feedback: accuracy versus, 29; dependent variable for, 27; distraction and 107; emotions and, 25; enjoyment measures in, *28*, 29, *29*; entertainment measures in, 27, *32*, *33*; independent variable for, 27; meaningfulness measures in, *30*, 31; positive/negative feedback *versus*, 23, 41, 116; video games and, 14

Ariely, D., 7

attention, to task, 103, 106, 108

attitude: toward content, 109–11; toward games, 103, 105–8, 114, 115

authority cue, of message, 89, 99

About the Author

Ryan Rogers is an independent researcher living in Brooklyn, New York. He is the author of over twenty peer-reviewed publications, editor of *Understanding Esports: An Introduction to the Global Phenomenon*, and author of *How Video Games Impact Players: The Pitfalls and Benefits of a Gaming Society*. He has a Ph.D. from the University of North Carolina at Chapel Hill.

www.ingramcontent.com/pod-product-compliance
Lightning Source LLC
Chambersburg PA
CBHW022317280326
41932CB00010B/1135